Computer-Assisted
AUDITING
with MICROSOFT® GREAT PLAINS
Dynamics

Mark W. Lehman *Mississippi State University*

THOMSON
─★─ ™
SOUTH-WESTERN

Australia · Canada · Mexico · Singapore · Spain · United Kingdom · United States

THOMSON
™
SOUTH-WESTERN

Computer-Assisted Auditing with Microsoft® Great Plains Dynamics, 1e
Mark W. Lehman

Editor-in-Chief:
Jack Calhoun

Team Leader:
Melissa Acuna

Acquisitions Editor:
Sharon Oblinger

Developmental Editor:
Erin McGraw

Marketing Manager:
Julie Lindsay

Production Editor:
Erin McGraw

Manufacturing Coordinator:
Doug Wilke

Compositor:
DPS Associates, Inc.

Printer:
Transcontinental Printing
Peterborough, Canada

Internal Designer:
Casey Gilbertson

Cover Designer:
Casey Gilbertson

COPYRIGHT © 2003
by South-Western, a division of
Thomson Learning. Thomson
Learning™ is a registered trademark
used herein under license.

Printed in Canada
  2 3 4 5 04

For more information
contact South-Western,
5191 Natorp Boulevard,
Mason, Ohio, 45040
or you can visit our Internet site
at: http://www.swcollege.com

ALL RIGHTS RESERVED.
No part of this work covered by
the copyright hereon may be
reproduced or used in any form
or by any means—graphic,
electronic, or mechanical,
including photocopying,
recording, taping, Web
distribution or information
storage and retrieval systems—
without the written permission of
the publisher.

For permission to use material
from this text or product, contact
us by
Telephone: 800-730-2214
Fax: 800-730-2215
http://www.thomsonrights.com

Library of Congress Cataloging-
in-Publication Data
Lehman, Mark W.
Computer-assisted auditing with
Microsoft® Great Plains dynamics/
by Mark W. Lehman.—1st ed.
p. cm.
Includes index.
ISBN 0-324-26961-7
1. Accounting—Computer-
assisted instruction—Software. 2.
Accounting—Software.
I. Title

HF5679.L367 2002
657'.45'02855369—dc21
2001057718

Contents

Preface

Students entering the auditing profession today must be prepared to utilize computer technology efficiently. As more clients adopt today's enterprise resource planning (ERP) software, entry-level auditors must possess the skills to obtain data directly from the client's ERP system and analyze that data using spreadsheet and database software.

This book provides you the opportunity to audit a client using a current, fully functional ERP system—Microsoft® Great Plains Dynamics. Dynamics is one of several ERP systems offered by Microsoft® Great Plains Business Solutions, a wholly owned subsidiary of Microsoft, Inc. The software is targeted to small to mid-sized companies operating on Microsoft technologies. For information about Dynamics, visit http://www.greatplains.com.

The projects in this book guide you through testing Southern Landscape, Inc. (SLI), a hypothetical company with over 1,400 transactions. Hidden among these transactions are a wide variety of questionable transactions, errors, and frauds.

USING THIS TEXTBOOK

The book contains the following sections and supplemental materials.

- **Tutorial.** You will learn to use the common features and commands of Dynamics, including Inquiry, Reports, Cards, and Explorer. The tutorial uses The World Online, Inc., the sample company provided with Dynamics.
- **Company Profile.** The profile presents a history of SLI, introduces the board of directors and employees, describes issues related to selected accounts, and concludes with management's discussion and analysis of the audit fiscal year's operations.
- **Projects.** Each of the 15 projects begins with a statement of the audit objective. A brief discussion of the typical audit procedures follows. You will then search for the data required to gather the required audit evidence. For many projects, the data accessed using Dynamics' Explorer are analyzed further using Microsoft Excel tools, including:
    - AutoFilter
    - Consolidation
    - Sort
    - PivotTable
    - Charts
    - Advanced Filter

  One project illustrates how data can be imported into Access for further analysis using select and crosstab queries. Another project merges data with a Word document. Each project concludes with a short series of questions.
- **Instructor's Manual.** The Instructor's Manual contains solutions to all project questions and examination questions for each project.

STUDENT COMPUTER SKILLS REQUIREMENTS

Today's accounting students should possess ample technology skills to complete these projects. The instructions assume you have experience using any Windows-based software and, therefore, are comfortable using the mouse to select menu options, toolbar buttons, and open and close windows. For projects including data analysis using Excel, you should be able to open a blank workbook, insert rows, format cells, select worksheets, create formulas, print, and save. Project instructions for advanced Excel features are detailed and are accompanied by screen images.

Project #15 uses Access to search for unusual relationships in sales transactions. The instructions for this project are very detailed, assuming you have no prior experience with a relational database. Project #3 uses Word to merge accounts receivable data with a form letter. The project instructions assume you have a basic knowledge of word processing and provide detailed instructions for merging the documents.

SYSTEM REQUIREMENTS

The minimum hardware requirements for this installation of Dynamics include:

- Windows 95
- Intel Pentium 166
- 250 MB hard disk space
- 64MB RAM
- SVGA (800 × 600) with 16-bit video driver
- CD-ROM
- Floppy disk drive

ACKNOWLEDGEMENTS

I wish to thank Fred Shaidnagle for his efforts to ensure that the projects reflect realistic auditing procedures in an ERP environment. I also wish to thank the individuals who worked on this project: Blair Pyron, my student assistant, and Erin McGraw and Sharon Oblinger of South-Western Publishing. Finally, thank you to Kristin Andersen and Janelle Daugherty of Microsoft® Great Plains for their efforts to assist accounting professors to incorporate ERP applications.

Microsoft® Great Plains Dynamics Audit Staff Tutorial

In your role as a first-year staff auditor, you are likely to be assigned to an audit engagement with a client that uses an enterprise resource planning (ERP) system such as Microsoft Great Plains Dynamics. These clients expect audit staff to obtain audit evidence directly from the ERP system. This tutorial will teach you how to use Dynamics to acquire the audit evidence necessary to complete selected audit procedures.

Dynamics is an ERP system designed for small to medium-sized businesses. An ERP system is a collection of related business application software that share data stored in a single database. A typical ERP supports numerous business applications, including marketing, sales, production, procurement, human resources, financial reporting, and fixed asset management. Thus, employees in virtually every functional area of the business will regularly interact with the ERP system.

Dynamics consists of a core financial module for recording common accounting transactions, such as sales and purchases, and the preparation of financial statements and managerial reports. Optional modules can be added to handle more unique information needs, such as human resources, fixed asset management, and production management. Thus, a Dynamics system is tailored to each client's needs and may vary in some respects.

This tutorial will provide you with a basic knowledge of Dynamics features. Armed with this knowledge, you should be able to quickly learn any unique features of a client's system.

You may have previously learned how to use Dynamics or another ERP system from a user perspective. Your training would have focused on entering transactions. As an auditor, however, your focus is different. Rather than entering transactions, you are examining transactions that have already been entered. Thus, this tutorial focuses on the procedures for accessing transaction information, both individually and collectively.

COMMAND NOTATIONS

Before you begin, examine the following instruction formats used in this tutorial.

- Menu commands will be represented in bold print separated by the **>>** sign.
  Example: **1** Select **Transactions >> Sales >> Invoice Entry**.

- Text or numbers to be entered are displayed in bold print. The statement will typically identify the label of the box where the item should be entered.
  Examples: **5** Enter **1423.23** in the Amount box.

  6 Select the type **Profit and Loss**.

- Buttons are displayed in bold. The statement will instruct you to click on the button name or may use the button name in the sentence.

  Examples: **3** Click **Columns** to add the Credit Limit column.

  4 Export the search results to **Excel**.

  5 **Save** the report format.

LOG-ON PROCEDURES

To start Dynamics:

1 Install Dynamics from the enclosed CDs.

2 Click **Start** on the Windows task bar.

3 Select **Programs >> Great Plains Dynamics 6.0 Student Audit >> Great Plains Dynamics** to display the Welcome to Great Plains Dynamics window in Figure T.1.

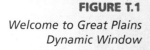
FIGURE T.1
Welcome to Great Plains Dynamic Window

To log on to Dynamics:

1 Enter **auditors** in the User ID box.

2 Enter **dynamics** in the Password box.

3 Click **OK.** The Company Log on window shown in Figure T.2 appears.

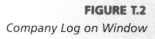
FIGURE T.2
Company Log on Window

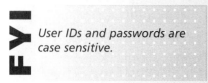
User IDs and passwords are case sensitive.

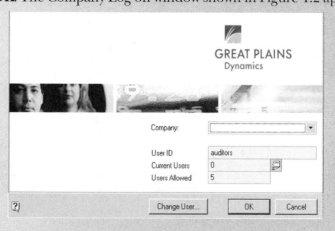

To select the company:

1 Select **The World Online, Inc.** in the Company box and click **OK**. The Dynamics main menu in Figure T.3 appears.

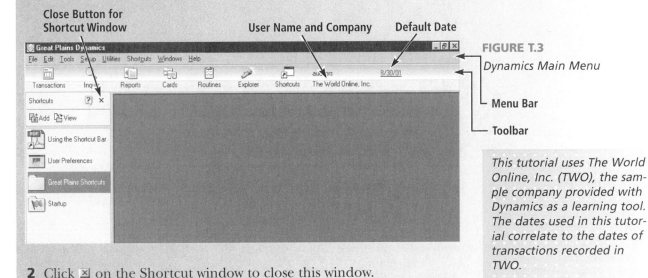

Close Button for Shortcut Window

User Name and Company   **Default Date**

FIGURE T.3

Dynamics Main Menu

Menu Bar

Toolbar

This tutorial uses The World Online, Inc. (TWO), the sample company provided with Dynamics as a learning tool. The dates used in this tutorial correlate to the dates of transactions recorded in TWO.

2 Click ⊠ on the Shortcut window to close this window.

Examine the components of the main menu. Consistent with other Windows-based software, commands can be accessed through a menu bar or toolbar. The user name, company, and default date are displayed to the right of the toolbar.

This default date is especially useful for individuals entering transactions. Although the auditor is not entering transactions, changing the default date to the interim audit date or fiscal year end date may be required to access the desired data.

To change the default date:

1 Click on the date to display a User Date window similar to Figure T.4.

2 Enter **12311999** and click **OK**.

FIGURE T.4

User Date Window

The date is entered in MMDDYYYY format where MM is the month, DD is the day, and YYYY is the year.

SELECTING COMMANDS

Clicking an item on the menu bar or toolbar reveals a list of items called a *palette*, such as the Transaction palette shown to the right. Selecting a palette item can execute a specific Dynamics feature or reveal another palette with more detailed selections.

Financial
Sales
Purchasing
Inventory
Payroll
Payroll - Canada
Project
Manufacturing
Fixed Assets

Sales Transactions	⊣
Transaction Entry
Cash Receipts
Apply
Series Post
Posted Transactions
Edit Trx Information
Receivables Batches
Invoicing Batches
Invoice Entry
Sales Batches
Sales Trx Entry
Print Sales Docs
Holds Processing
Order Fulfillment

The following tasks illustrate how to use the menu bar and toolbar.

Task #1—Using a menu bar command, select your printer:

1 Select **File >> Print Setup** to display the typical Windows Print Setup window.

2 Select a printer in the Name box and click **OK**.

Task #2—Using a toolbar command, examine the window to enter sales transactions:

1 Select **Transaction >> Sales** to view the Sales Transactions palette shown at the left.

2 Select **Sales Trx Entry** to display the Sales Transaction Entry window.

3 Click ⊠ in the upper right corner of the Sales Transaction Entry window to close the window.

FYI

Notice that the Sales Transaction palette also closed when the Sales Transaction Entry window was closed. Palettes typically close after you select them. If you are repeatedly making selections from a palette, you may want the palette to remain on the desktop. To keep the palette on the desktop, click the Push-pin button once. The button will change as shown below indicating that the palette is in the "pinned" position. To allow the palette to close, simply click the button once. 📌

Every window has a ⊠ Close button in the upper right corner of the window. If instructed to "Close a window," click on the ⊠ button.

ACCESSING TRANSACTION DATA

Auditors often need to examine detailed information regarding financial transactions and account activity. The Inquiry feature on the toolbar is a versatile tool for examining this information. This section introduces you to the Inquiry feature and several tools common to many Dynamics windows.

Suppose you needed to examine information related to a specific sales transaction. To view the transaction using the Inquiry feature:

1 Select **Inquiry >> Sales >> Trx by Document** to display the Receivables Transaction Inquiry—Document window shown in Figure T.5. *Leave this screen open for the exercises in this section.*

FIGURE T.5

Receivables Transaction Inquiry— Document Window

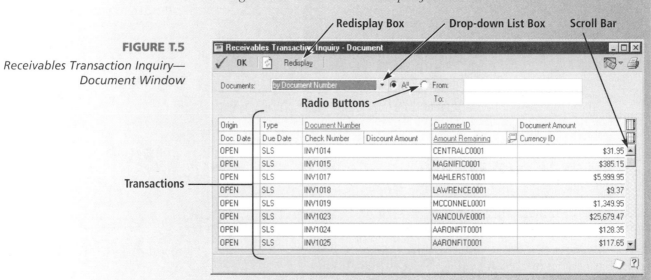

Redisplay Box   Drop-down List Box   Scroll Bar

Radio Buttons

Transactions

The window displays one line of detail for each transaction. The scroll bar is used to move down the list.

Drop-down List Boxes

The Documents box is an example of a Drop-down List box, as indicated by the down arrow button at the right corner of the box. A Drop-down List box enables you to select an option from a list.

To practice using a Drop-down List box:

1 Click anywhere within the Documents box to reveal the list.

2 Select **by Document Date**.

Radio Buttons

The All and From buttons in Figure T.5 are examples of Radio buttons. A Radio button is used to select an option from a list displayed on the screen. The option is selected when the button is filled. Clicking on the button selects or deselects the option.

If the All button is filled, Inquiry displays all the documents. If the From button is filled, you can enter a range of documents to be displayed.

To practice using a Radio button:

1 Click on the **From** Radio button.

2 Enter **01011999** in the From box.

3 Enter **01081999** in the To box.

4 Click **Redisplay** to display only the transactions between these dates.

Lookup Buttons

Auditors frequently seek information on a particular item, such as a customer, vendor, document, or account. Rather than entering the item using the keyboard, you can select the item from a list using a Lookup button.

To practice using a Lookup button:

1 Select **by Customer ID** in the Documents Drop-down List box. Notice that Lookup buttons appear in the From and To boxes, as shown in Figure T.6.

FIGURE T.6

*Receivables Transaction
Inquiry—Document Window*

Zoom Features   Lookup Buttons   Show and Hide
Buttons

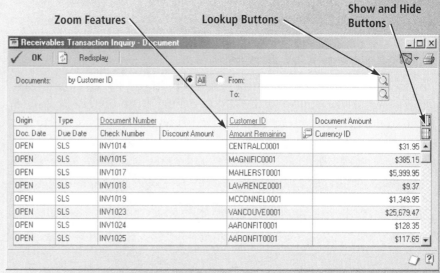

2 Click the **Lookup** button for the From box to view the Customer and
Prospects window shown in Figure T.7.

FIGURE T.7

*Customer and Prospects
Window*

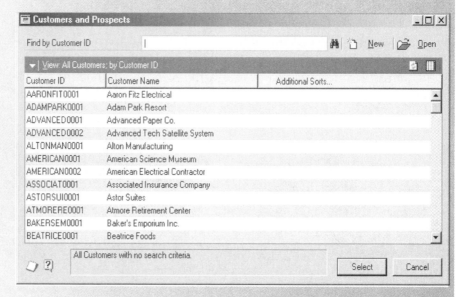

3 Select the account for **Beatrice Foods** (highlight the account and
click **Select**, or simply double-click on the account).

4 Click **Redisplay** to revise the list to display all Beatrice Foods transactions.

Notice that entering data in the From box automatically selected the
From Radio button. Dynamics also entered the account in the To box,
assuming that you want to view the activity for only a single account.

Show and Hide Buttons

The window in Figure T.6 shows a single line of data for each transaction. The data corresponds to the fields listed in the first line of the
header section. The Show and Hide buttons modify the number of

items displayed for each transaction. The Hide button reveals only the first line of information for each item. The Show button displays additional lines of information.

To practice using the Show and Hide buttons:

1 Click **Show** to view two lines of data for each document, as shown in Figure T.8.

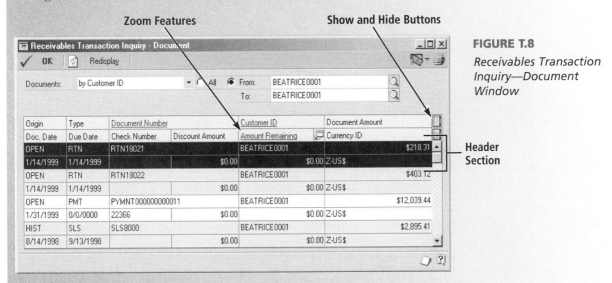

FIGURE T.8

Receivables Transaction Inquiry—Document Window

Notice that the background color of the first two lines is black, indicating that both lines display information regarding document number RTN18021. Subsequent pairs of lines are displayed in alternating backgrounds to visually differentiate the information for each document.

2 Click **Hide** to display one line of data for each document.

Zoom Feature

After viewing a list of items, the auditor may desire to view detailed information related to a single item. The Zoom feature enables you to view detailed information for the selected item. Unlike other Dynamics features, the Zoom feature is not represented by an icon or button. Rather, as shown in Figure T.8, the Zoom feature is an underlined item description in a form header. The window in Figure T.8 has three Zoom features: Document Number, Customer ID, and Amount Remaining.

To practice using the Zoom feature:

1 Select document number **SLS8000**.

2 Click **Customer ID** (see Figure T.8) to view the Customer Inquiry window shown in Figure T.9.

3 After examining detailed information about the customer, click **OK**.

Distribution   **Distribution Button**

The account distribution for each transaction can be determined by many factors. For example, the account distribution of a sales transaction depends on the customer and the parts sold (if any). You can examine the account distribution assigned to any transaction using the Distributions button.

To practice using the Distribution button:

1 Click **Document Number** in the header section to view the Receivables Transaction Inquiry Zoom window shown in Figure T.10.

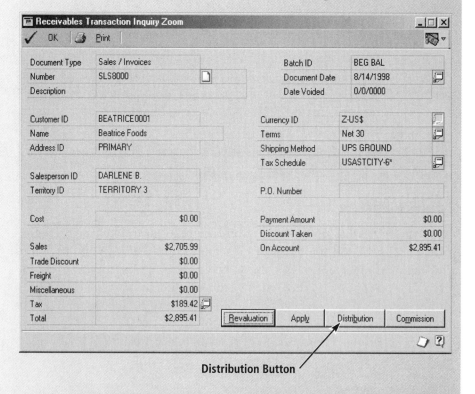

Distribution Button

2 Click **Distribution** to view the Receivables Distribution Inquiry Zoom window.

3 After examining the account distribution, click **OK** three times to close all the open windows.

ACCESSING MASTER DATA

Master data is relatively permanent information related to an individual item, such as a customer, employee, inventory item, or account. The Cards feature is an effective tool for obtaining data related to master data. This section will introduce you to the Cards feature and two new Dynamics commands.

Navigation Buttons

Use the Navigation buttons to scroll through records of the selected item, such as customers, vendors, and inventory items. Resembling buttons commonly found on electronic equipment, the Navigation buttons are especially useful when you do not know the item you want to access, allowing you to scan the records.

|◄ First Record   ► Next Record

◄ Previous Record   ►| Last Record

To practice using the Navigation buttons:

1 Select **Cards >> Inventory >> Item** to display the Item Maintenance window in Figure T.11.

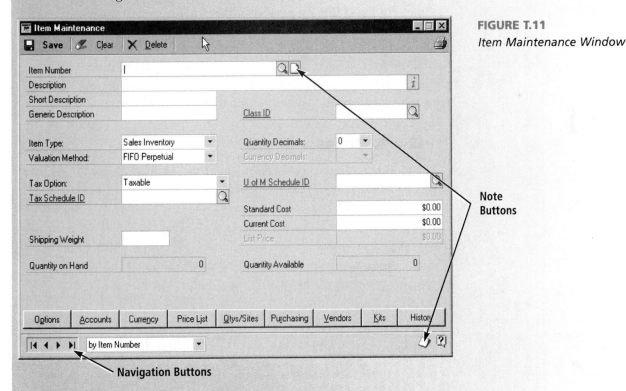

FIGURE T.11
Item Maintenance Window

2 Click **Next Record** twice to view item number 128 SDRAM.

3 Click **Last Record** to view item number WIRE100.

Notes can be attached to data or windows. Notice that Figure T.11 has two Note buttons. The Note button adjacent to the item number would store a note related to that item. The Note button in the lower right corner of the window would store a note related to the Item Maintenance window.

 Note Buttons

Dynamics provides the user with data entry fields for a wide range of data related to the item. Regardless, data may need to be captured that does not "fit" in any existing data entry field. The Note button displays a window that enables the user to enter any additional data pertinent to the item. While performing audit procedures, the auditor may elect to check the Note window for any pertinent information related to the item being examined.

To practice using a Note button:

1 Click the **Note** button adjacent to the Item Number box to view a Note window. *There is no text added to this note.*

2 **Close** all open windows.

You can determine if a note is recorded by examining the color of the Note button. The button color is yellow if a note is attached.

CREATING REPORTS

The Inquiry and Cards features are effective tools for performing online inquiries. For queries resulting in printed reports, the Report feature on the toolbar is the preferred tool. The Reports feature contains numerous preformatted reports, such as financial statements. Selecting from a variety of available options enables you to customize the report to contain the data of interest. This section will teach you how to create a report and introduce you to check boxes.

☑ Check Boxes

A Check box is similar to the Radio button. A Check box enables you to select an option displayed on the screen.

Unlike Radio buttons, several Check boxes within a group can be checked. When printing a report, for example, you can select to display the report on the screen, print a copy on the printer, and save the report to a file.

To practice using a Check box:

1 Select **Reports >> Financial >> Financial Statements** to display the Financial Statement Report window in Figure T.12.

2 Select **Profit and Loss** in the Report box (use the Lookup button).

3 Click **New** to view the Financial Statement Report Options window in Figure T.13.

4 Enter **Audit Income Statement** in the Option box.

5 Select **Summary** in the Amounts box (use the Drop-down list).

6 Select **Account** in the Segment ID box (use the the Lookup button).

7 Select account **1100** in the From box (use the Lookup button).

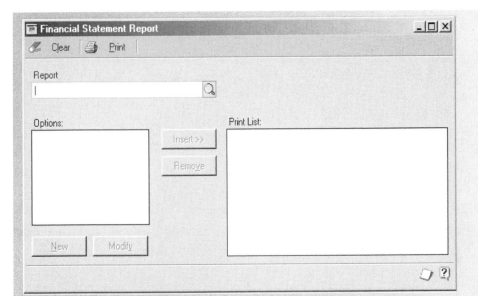

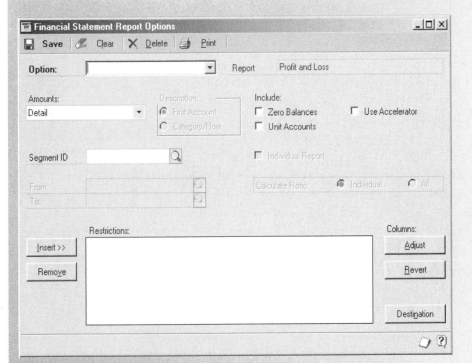

8 Select account **9999** in the To box (use the Lookup button).

9 Click **Insert** to enter information in the Restrictions box.

10 Click **Destination** to view the Report Destination window shown in Figure T.14.

11 Click the **Screen** Check box to display the report to the screen.

12 Click the **Printer** Check box to remove the check, thus precluding the report from being printed to the screen.

13 Click the **File** Check box to print the report to a file.

14 Enter **Audit Income Statement.html** in the File Name box.

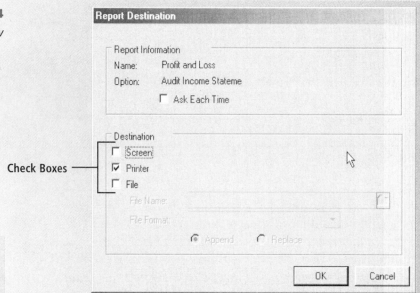

Check Boxes

The html extension must be included in the file name even though the html file format is selected.

15 Select **html** in the File Format box. Your Report Destination window should now appear as shown in Figure T.15.

The file will be saved in the C:\Program Files\Great Plains Dynamics 6.0 Student Audit folder. Or, you can use the folder icon adjacent to the file name box to save the file to an alternate location.

16 Click **OK** to close the Report Destination window.

17 Click **Print** to display the report and save a copy to a disk file.

18 **Close** the Screen Output window and click **Save** to save the report format.

19 **Close** the Financial Statement Report Options and Financial Statement Report windows.

Explorer

Explorer

Audit procedures often require the auditor to analyze a large number of transactions. For example, auditors frequently search cash expenditures for checks written to related parties. Performing such a search using either the Inquiry or Cards features would be impractical.

The Explorer is a powerful feature that enables the auditor to create and save custom views of system data. The output is presented in a database format that can be imported by spreadsheet, word processing, and database software. Explorer lets you select the data items to be included in the output, sort the data, and select records that meet specified criteria. This section teaches you how to create an Explorer inquiry and to import the output into an Excel spreadsheet.

Suppose that you, in preparation for a physical inventory observation, desire to have a list of items costing more than $1,000. The following steps illustrate how to create this view.

Explorer has 26 predefined search criteria called objects. *Each object has a default search, or view, that displays only a small number of the available data items. Using the default view as a starting point, you can create a custom view by changing the data items, sorting the data, and selecting records that meet a variety of criteria. Saving the view allows you quick access to the data.*

To begin creating an Explorer view:

1 Select **Explorer** to view the Explorer window in Figure T.16.

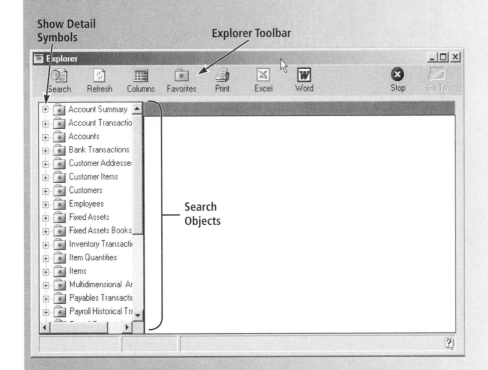

FIGURE T.16
Explorer Window

2 Click **Items** in the Search Objects window.

3 Click the **Show Detail** symbol adjacent to the Items search object to show the expanded search object list shown in Figure T.17.

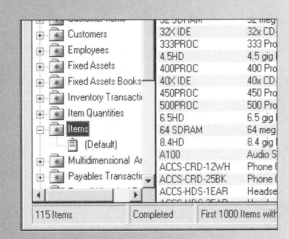

FIGURE T.17
Items Object Expanded

The Show Detail symbol, ⊞, shows the default and custom views of a search object. The Hide Detail symbol, ⊟, closes the detail.

4 Click **Default** to display the search results shown in Figure T.18.

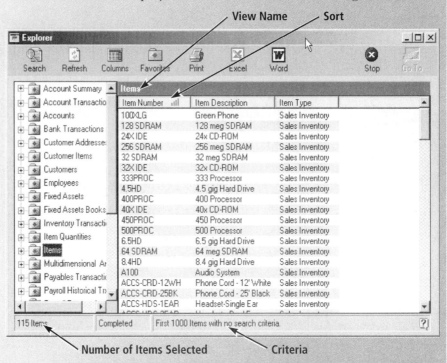

The Explorer window displays the following information about the search results:

Columns	The view currently contains three columns: Item Number, Item Description, and Item Type.
Sort	The icon adjacent to the Item Number column heading ▁ indicates that the search results are sorted in ascending order by Item Number. Sorting the search results in descending order is denoted by the ▁ symbol.
Criteria	There are no criteria limiting the items in the list. The search results are the first 1,000 records.
Number of Items Selected	The entire list of inventory, 115 items, is currently displayed.

To change the columns in the query:

5 Select **Columns** on the Explorer toolbar to display the Change Column Display window in Figure T.19.

6 Click **Add** to display the Columns window in Figure T.20.

7 Select the **Current Cost** field (select the field and click **OK** or double-click on the field).

8 Click on the **Item Type** field in the Change Column Display window.

9 Click **Remove** to delete the column.

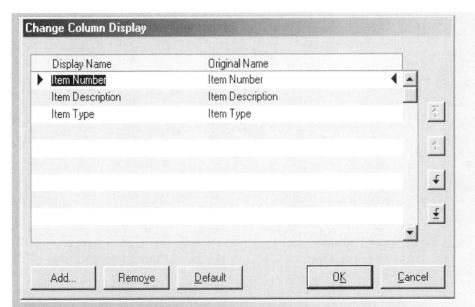

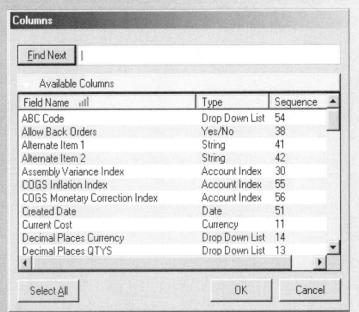

FIGURE T.20

Columns Window

The Columns window displays every field having data related to inventory items. The size of the list illustrates the wide array of data that can be stored by an ERP system.

FYI

10 Click **OK** to run to revised view.

To sort the items:

11 Click the **Current Cost** column heading once to sort the list in ascending order by Current Cost.

12 Click the **Current Cost** column heading again to sort the list in descending order by Current Cost.

To limit the records selected:

13 Select **Search** on the Explorer toolbar to view the Search Items window in Figure T.21.

14 Select **Current Cost** in the first field box (use the Lookup button) and click **OK**.

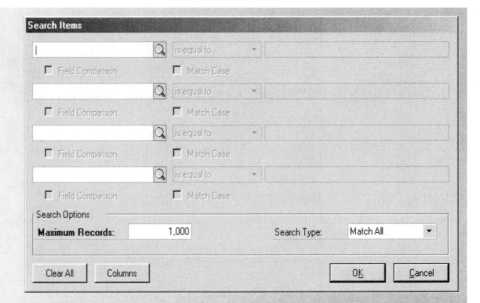

15 Select **is greater than** in the first criteria box (use the Drop-down List button).

16 Enter **1000** in the first data box.

17 Click **OK**.

To export the search results to Excel:

18 Open a blank notebook in Excel.

19 In Dynamics, select **Excel** on the Explorer toolbar. The data will be exported to the blank Excel notebook.

20 Save the Excel notebook as **High Cost Items**.

To save the view for use in future audits:

21 In Dynamics, click **Favorites** on the Explorer toolbar.

22 Enter **High Cost Items** in the Name box.

23 Select **User ID** in the Visible To box, enabling only the auditor to access the view.

24 Click **Add**.

25 Click **Show Detail** for Items to confirm that your view is saved. The view is now available for subsequent audit engagements.

FEATURE REVIEW

This tutorial has introduced a variety of icons and buttons that are used on Dynamics windows. The table on the following page summarizes these items.

Button or Icon	Title	Description
⊠	Close	The standard Windows icon to close a window, the Close button is located in the upper right corner of the window.
▾	Drop-down List	Adjacent to a text box, a Drop-down List box displays a list of available options.
◉	Radio	Clicking a Radio button selects the feature described by the adjacent text. Radio buttons are typically in a group, where only a single button can be selected at any time.
🔍	Lookup	Adjacent to a text box, a Lookup button displays a window containing a list of items stored in the system.
▦	Show	Positioned to the right of headings of transaction windows, the Show button displays two or more lines of information for each item.
▥	Hide	Positioned to the right of headings of transaction windows, the Hide button displays one line of information for each item.
Distribution	Distribution	A button positioned on many transaction windows, the Distribution button displays the account distribution of the transaction.
📝	Notes	This displays a window containing information related to the item or transaction. The icon changes to yellow if a note is attached to the item or transaction.
☑	Check	Clicking a Check box selects the feature described by the adjacent text. If several Check buttons are presented in a group, two or more of the related features can be selected.
⏹	Explorer Sort	This symbol adjacent to a column heading indicates the column and order into which the data is sorted.
Redisplay	Redisplay	The Redisplay button displays the transactions or items selected by options entered on an inquiry window.
OK	OK	A button found on many windows, the OK button processes the data and options entered on the window.

TEST YOUR SKILLS

. . . .

This tutorial has provided you a brief introduction to the Dynamics features you will use to obtain audit evidence. Complete the following tasks to test your knowledge of these basic skills.

Task # 1—Identify the number of invoices from Associated Insurance Inc.

1 Select **Inquiry >> Purchasing >> Trx by Vendor**.

2 Select **Associated Insurance Inc.** in the Vendor ID box.

Answer: Four invoices (Type equals INV) and three payments (Type equals PMT) appear on the Payments Transactions Inquiry—Vendor window.

Task # 2—Determine the name and amount of the largest payment received from 12/30/1998 to 1/2/1999.

1 Select **Inquiry >> Sales >> Trx by Document**.

2 Select **by Document Date** in the Documents box.

3 Enter **12301998** in the From box.

4 Enter **01021999** in the To box.

5 Click **Redisplay** to display the transactions.

6 Click **Show** to display the transaction details. Search the list for transactions have a Type equal to PMT and an amount in the Document Amount box.

Answer: National Shopping World paid $11,404.87 on 1/2/1999.

Task # 3—Determine the debit account number(s) for the invoice from Vista Travel.

1 Select **Inquiry >> Purchasing >> Trx by Vendor**.

2 Select **Vista Travel** in the Vendor ID box.

3 Make sure the transaction is selected.

4 Click **Document Number** to view the transaction details.

5 Click **Distribution** to view the account distribution.

Answer: Accounts 300-6520-00 and 000-6630-00.

Task # 4—Determine the account title for account 000-6630-00.

1 Select **Cards >> Financial >> Account**.

2 Select **000-6630-00** in the Account box.

Answer: IL State Sales Tax Expense.

Task # 5—Determine the quantity available of item PHON-BUS-1250.

1 Select **Cards >> Inventory >> Item**.

2 Select **PHON-BUS-1250** in the Item Number box.

Answer: 271

Task # 6—Prepare a balance sheet as of 12/31/1999.

1 Select **Reports >> Financial >> Financial Statements**.
2 Select **Balance Sheet** in the Report box.
3 Click **New** to create a new report format.
4 Enter the option name **Sample Balance Sheet**.
5 Select **Account** in the Segment ID box.
6 Select all accounts in the From and To boxes.
7 Click **Insert** to enter the segment information in the Restrictions box.
8 Click **Destination** and change the report destination to screen only.
9 Click **OK** and **Print** to view the report on the screen.

Answer: Total assets equal $4,093,660.52.

Task # 7—Create an Excel file containing a list of all fixed assets with an acquisition cost greater than $10,000. Sort the list in descending order by the acquisition cost.

1 Select **Explorer >> Fixed Assets >> Default**.
2 Click **Search** to enter the criteria **Acquisition Cost is greater than 10000**.
3 Export the search results to **Excel**.

Answer: Nine assets are selected.

Task # 8—Create an Excel file containing a list of all sales/invoices to customers who have an outstanding 91-120 days past due balance of more than $10,000.

1 Select **Explorer >> Receivable Transactions >> Default**.
2 Click **Columns** to add the **91-120 Days** column.
3 Click **Search** to enter the following criteria:
  a **91-120 Days is greater than 10000**.
  b **Document Type is equal to Sales/Invoices**.
4 Export the search results to **Excel**.

Answer: Three customers having 14 sales/invoices are selected.

PROJECT INSTRUCTIONS

The projects in this text contain instructions that resemble those in the eight tasks you just completed. The instructions identify the Dynamics tools you will use. You are expected to know when and how to use the tools in the Feature Review of this tutorial. For example, project instructions assumes you know how to use a Lookup button to select a vendor or account. The instructions also assume you will close open windows and palettes before beginning the next task.

Some projects require you to perform some advanced features using Microsoft Excel, Word, and Access. The instructions for these tasks, such as the Excel consolidation feature, are very detailed and are accompanied by figures. The instructions assume you can perform fundamental Excel and Word tasks, such as inserting rows, creating formulas, formatting, save, and print. The instructions assume you have little prior knowledge of Access.

Begin each project by starting Dynamics and logging in to the system using **auditors** as the User ID and **dynamics** as the password. Unless instructed otherwise, modify the user date to 12/31/2002. Select Southern Landscape, Inc., as the company.

PREPARE TO AUDIT

Generally accepted auditing standards state that audit evidence is gathered through observation, inspection, confirmation, and inquiry. Visualize these methods as tools within an auditor's toolbox. In planning an audit, the auditor must consider which tools will provide the sufficient and competent audit evidence necessary to support a particular financial statement assertion. Dynamics' inquiry, reports, cards, and Explorer features provide the auditor with powerful tools for gathering audit evidence.

Obtaining audit evidence for a particular assertion typically requires the use of several audit tools. Consider the assertion that inventory is valued at the lower of cost or market. To test this assertion, the auditor will search for the existence of obsolete inventory items. The auditor can use Explorer to prepare a list of inventory items that have not sold in several months. Based solely on this information, should the auditor recommend that these items be written off? No, the auditor must also obtain inquiry evidence from client personnel. This example illustrates that Dynamics' tools make the process of gathering some audit evidence more effective and efficient, but that Dynamics tools cannot be relied upon as the sole source of audit evidence.

The 15 projects in this textbook are designed to illustrate how an auditor can gather audit evidence using an ERP system. These projects do not, however, represent a complete list of all the audit procedures that can be performed with Dynamics or would be performed in a real audit engagement. The auditor must possess a sufficient knowledge of Dynamics and the client's operations to design a comprehensive audit plan that includes gathering data using Dynamics' tools.

Company Profile for Southern Landscape, Inc.

Southern Landscape, Inc. (SLI) was initially organized as a sole proprietorship by John Patrick and began business in 1967 as Farm Supply Company. Through the mid 1980s the company operated using its original business model, selling supplies to farmers and ranchers in the four-county area surrounding Columbus, Mississippi.

In 1985 the company experienced a transformation when the business was incorporated and John Patrick turned over the daily business operations to his son Stephen. The new business also adopted a new target market. Building on its successes, the SLI expanded its product line to include landscaping products marketed to individuals, contractors, and retail businesses.

SALES

The company currently operates from a single location in Columbus. The main sales building (the store) contains most of the inventory, sales counters, and administrative offices. Plants are housed in a greenhouse adjacent to the sales building. A separate drive-through warehouse stores bulk feeds, fertilizers, and chemicals.

Except for nursery and warehouse items, customers select their items and check out with an employee located at the store entrance. For items stored in the warehouse, customers receive a copy of the sales invoice presented to warehouse workers to fill the order. Customers drive through the middle of the warehouse, where warehouse workers load the items printed on the sales invoice.

EMPLOYEES

When the company was incorporated, stock was sold to several individuals outside of the Patrick family. The funds were used to construct the store and the adjacent greenhouse. Because of a lack of segregation of duties, the minority stockholders have required an annual financial statement audit. At the request of the board of directors, the audit typically contains some audit procedures designed to detect fraudulent activities and related party transactions.

The names of the individuals comprising the Board of Directors are listed below:

Name	Position/Profession	Stock Ownership
John Patrick	Chairman	25%
Carol Patrick	Retired	25%
Thomas Blette	Partner in law firm of Smith, Blette & Harris	20%
Janice Kellogg	Managing partner of Kellogg & Associates, LLC	10%
F. Daniel Frank	Owner, Southern Hills Farming	10%
Sanders Crabtree	Professor, Central State University, Department of Horticulture	—

Most of SLI's employees have been with the company for many years. Unlike similar retail businesses, John Patrick has been able to retain his employees by offering them a competitive package that includes an annual salary, vacation time, and medical benefits.

Stephen Patrick, Manager, 10% owner. Stephen, the son of John and Carol Patrick, is responsible for the daily operations of the business. Stephen orders inventory, manages personnel, and oversees the sales operations. During high school and college, Stephen worked a variety of jobs with farmers, ranchers, and landscape architects to gain first-hand knowledge of SLI's primary customers. After completing his degree in horticulture from Central State University, he began working at SLI and assumed complete responsibility for the company when he was 30 years old.

John Matthews, Business Manager. John is a college friend of Stephen Patrick. He received a marketing degree with an accounting minor from Central State University. Upon graduation he accepted a position in the data processing department of a local business and advanced to the position of systems analyst. On the strength of his computer knowledge, John was hired in 2001 to install and operate Dynamics. He is totally responsible for the accounting system, preparation of checks, cash management, and financial statement preparation.

Ken Clark, Sales Clerk. Ken is one of three full-time sales clerks. He joined SLI in 1996 after owning and operating a beef ranch for 30 years. Thus, Ken spends most of his time working with ranchers and farmers.

Daniel Rackley, Sales Clerk. Daniel works full time in the store. Daniel has worked with SLI for only one year, having recently worked with PWC Farming, one of SLI's best customers.

Mark Kelly, Sales Clerk. Mark has worked for SLI since 1992. He began as a warehouse worker before moving to a sales position in 1998.

Jeanne Berry, Nursery Manager. Jeanne has primary responsibility for the nursery and spends most of her time assisting customers there. Like Stephen Patrick, she is also a horticulture graduate of Central State University.

Randy Adams, Warehouse Manager. Randy has primary responsibility for the operations of the warehouse. He accepts and stocks received orders and fills orders as customers drive through the warehouse.

Chris Harrison, Warehouse Worker. Chris spends most of his time filling customer orders in the warehouse. He has worked for SLI since 1990.

STRATEGIC PLANS

The Board of Directors has authorized John Patrick to pursue a horizontal expansion plan. The plan authorizes the company to open stores in other major cities in Mississippi and Alabama, opening no more than one store per year. During 2002, Mr. Patrick spent most of his time investigating opportunities in two cities within a 60-mile radius of Columbus.

INSTALLATION OF GREAT PLAINS DYNAMICS

During the 1980s the company installed a computerized accounting system and point-of-sale cash registers. The point-of-sale system continues to meet the company's needs. However, the current accounting system is not adequate to handle the future growth needs of the company. Thus, in 2001 the company began the process of installing Great Plains Dynamics.

The transition from the legacy accounting system to Dynamics was completed on December 31, 2001. Year-end account balances including detailed records of accounts receivable, inventory, fixed assets, and payroll were recorded as of 12/31/01.

SLI is taking a phased approach to installing Dynamics. During 2002 the company began testing the interaction of the legacy point-of-sale system with Dynamics, with the goal of integrating the point-of-sale system on 12/31/2002 for the 2003 fiscal year. Until then, the transactions recorded by the point-of-sale system are being key-entered as a single weekly transaction.

To support the expansion plan, SLI adopted a three-segment general ledger account code in XXX-YYYY-ZZ format. The first three-digit segment will ultimately designate the store location. The last two-digit segment will be used to segregate costs by functions such as sales, marketing, purchasing, and corporate. During fiscal year 2002, only the middle four-digit segment was used. This segment designates the general ledger accounts.

ACCOUNT INFORMATION

Cash. SLI maintains two bank accounts. The First National Bank account is used for all cash receipts and expenditures except for payroll. The Union National Bank account is an imprest account for payroll and, therefore, maintains a zero book balance.

Accounts Receivable. SLI extends credit to a variety of customers, including farms, ranches, retail businesses, contractors, and schools. Credit terms are n/30 with a 1 percent per month finance charge for overdue accounts. Because 1 percent rate is a better rate than many customers can obtain with a bank loan, SLI's accounts receivable can often swell during the growing season. Based on local tax laws, schools are exempt from the state's 7 percent sales tax.

Inventory. The company uses the FIFO perpetual method to cost all of its inventory items. Based on local tax laws, some inventory items are not taxable; beef feed, for example, is not taxed because the item is considered a raw material used in the production of another taxable product.

SLI assigns each inventory item into one of four item classes:

Item Class	Common Items	Typical Markup
Farm	feeds, fencing, chemicals, seeds	20%
Nursery	bedding plants, trees	50%
Pet	cat and dog food	40%
Retail	hand tools, soils, clothing	50%

The four classes also have somewhat different cyclical sales patterns. Farm sales fluctuate during the year, with cattle items increasing during the winter months and crop items increasing during the spring. Nursery items are very cyclical, with bedding plants having a large spring season and a smaller fall season. Pet and retail sales are relatively constant during the year.

Fixed Assets. SLI segregates its fixed assets into four general ledger accounts: land, buildings, equipment, and transportation equipment.

Payroll. Employees are paid semi-monthly based on an annual salary. FICA, federal income, and state income taxes are withheld. The company maintains a health insurance policy. Employees pay a portion of the premiums through a payroll deduction, with the amount determined based on the number of dependents being deducted from each paycheck.

The employees also earn 80 hours of annual paid vacation. Unused vacation is carried forward to the next year.

MANAGEMENT DISCUSSION AND ANALYSIS

The following management discussion and analysis was prepared by Stephen Patrick at the request of the audit manager:

As expected, fiscal year 2002 reflected the same economic recession experienced in the prior year. Weather and commodity market conditions caused many farms and ranches to curtail their production, resulting in a significant decline in farm-related sales. Despite the relative decline in sales, SLI is committed to retaining its current employees to be strategically positioned to take advantage of the eventual upturn in business. As a result, the company incurred an unaudited operating loss of $262,720.48.

The installation of Dynamics proved to be more involved than expected. Ignoring the advice of Great Plains and its auditors, we did not engage a consultant to guide system implementation. John Matthews successfully argued that he had the knowledge required to install and operate the system. Despite John's best efforts, the system was not completely tested by the target January 1, 2002 implementation date. As a result, several problems occurred during the first quarter. Frustrated by these problems, John resigned during June and I assumed his job responsibilities.

Other factors contributed to the poor operating results. We significantly overestimated the number of trees that would be sold and continue to maintain a large inventory of these items. However, unlike bedding plants, unsold trees can survive the winter if properly maintained. The resultant unusually large inventory, combined with the continued downturn in sales, forced us to negotiate two bank loans.

We continued our practice of not recording accrual adjustments for the preparation of monthly financial statements. Given the current size of the company, the Board of Directors is satisfied with having monthly financial statements prepared on a modified accrual basis.

Project #1
Analytical Analysis in Audit Planning

AUDIT OBJECTIVE

Perform analytical procedures on interim financial statements to assess the level of audit risk and identify potential accounting and auditing issues.

STANDARD AUDIT PROCEDURE

Generally accepted auditing standards require that the auditor obtain sufficient competent evidential matter to afford a reasonable basis for an opinion. The auditor's perceived level of audit risk will influence the amount and nature of audit evidence to be obtained.

The analytical analysis of interim financial statements is one of several important sources of information the auditor uses to assess audit risk. One type of analytical analysis, referred to as trend analysis, compares interim financial statements to the prior year's financial statements and management budgets.

GATHERING EVIDENCE WITH DYNAMICS

Step 1: Prepare a comparative income statement.

SLI entered its 2002 annual budget and 2001 historical account balances for income statement accounts only. Use Dynamics to prepare a comparative income statement report. Dynamics' default income statement reports the current period and year-to-date amounts. You can modify the default report to add the year-to-date budget and historical amounts. The report can be saved to a file and imported into Excel for performing analytical analysis.

1 Select **Reports >> Financial >> Quick Financial**.

2 Select **Income Statement** in the Report box.

3 Select **Profit and Loss** in the Type box.

4 Select **YTD Budget** and click **Insert** to move the item to the Selected Columns box.

5 Select **FY2002** in the Budget ID box.

6 Select **YTD History** and click **Insert**.

7 Select **2001** in the History box.

8 **Save** the report format.

Having modified the income statement format, you can now print the report.

9 Modify the user date to **07/31/2002**.

10 Select **Reports >> Financial >> Financial Statements**.

11 Select the report **Income Statement**.

12 Click **New** to create a new report format.

13 Enter the option name **Audit Planning**.

14 Select the segment ID **Segment2**.

15 Enter segments from **1100** to **8010**.

16 **Insert** the segment information in the Restrictions box.

17 Click **Destination** and change the report destination to screen only.

18 Click **OK** and **Print** to view the report on the screen.

19 After viewing the report, close the Screen Output window.

20 Modify the report destination to print the report to a file, using a **Tab - delimited** file format, using the file name **Audit_Planning**.

21 **Print** the report to the file.

22 **Save** the report format.

FYI

Segment 2 refers to the middle section of an account number. Sales, for example, is account 000-4100-00.

Step 2: Prepare analytical analysis on the comparative income statement.

The comparative income statement can be imported into Excel to allow you to calculate a variety of financial ratios.

1 In Excel, open **Audit_Planning**.
In the Open dialog box, you will need to change the Files of type box to All Files. The text import wizard will automatically launch.

2 Ensure that the **Delimited** option is selected.

3 Use the scroll bar to identify the first row having a columnar structure. The column headings begin in row 7. Therefore, enter **7** in the Start import at row box. Your window should appear as shown in Figure 1.1.

4 Click **Next** to advance to the next window.

5 Ensure that the **Tab** delimiter is selected. Click **Finish**.

6 Modify the spreadsheet column widths as appropriate.

7 Delete unnecessary labels in rows.
The imported comparative income statement has headings on the top of each page. These headings, such as those found near row 40, need to be removed.

8 Add a column to calculate the percentage difference between the Current YTD and FY2002 YTD (the budget). Label the column **Actual-to-Budget YTD**.

FYI

*To enter the heading in column F, enter **Actual-to-Budget YTD** in F1. Highlight cells F1:F2 and select **Format>>Cells>>Alignment**. Click on the **Wrap text** and **Merge cells** check boxes. Increase the size of row 1, if necessary, to completely display the column heading.*

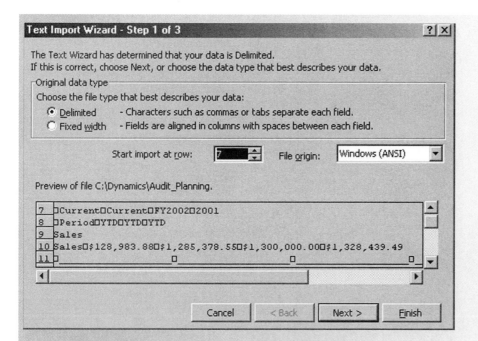

FIGURE 1.1

Excel Text Import Wizard, Window 1 of 3

9 Add a column to calculate the percentage difference between the Current YTD and 2001 YTD (historical). Label the column **Actual-to-History YTD**. Your spreadsheet should appear as shown in Figure 1.2.

FIGURE 1.2

Trend Analysis on Comparative Income Statement

	A	B	C	D	E	F	G
1		Current	Current	FY2002	2001	Actual-to-Budget	Actual-to-History
2		Period	YTD	YTD	YTD	YTD	YTD
3	Sales						
4	Sales	$128,983.88	$1,285,378.55	$1,300,000.00	$1,328,439.49	-1.1%	-3.2%
5							
6	Gross Sales	$128,983.88	$1,285,378.55	$1,300,000.00	$1,328,439.49	-1.1%	-3.2%
7	Sales Returns and Discounts						
8	Returns	$463.33	$8,741.20	$13,000.00	$8,746.26	-32.8%	-0.1%

10 Save the spreadsheet as an Excel file.

Step 3: Examine monthly budget information for a single account.

After completing the comparative income statement and analytical analysis, you may discover significant variations between actual and budget amounts for selected accounts. These differences reflect seven months of operations. The Inquiry tool can be used to obtain more detailed, monthly actual-to-budget information for any account.

1 In Dynamics, select **Inquiry >> Financial >> Budget vs. Actual**.

2 Select account **000-4100-00**.

3 Select **FY2002** in the Budget ID box to view the Budget vs Actual Inquiry window in Figure 1.3.

FIGURE 1.3

*Budget vs Actual
Inquiry Window*

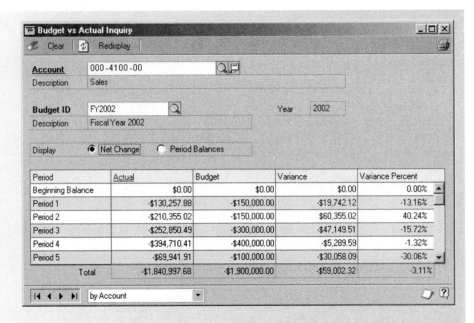

4 Select **File >> Print** to print the Inquiry window.

The Budget vs Actual Inquiry window presents the monthly variance amounts and percents. Analyzing the monthly variations provides you with detailed information that is useful when discussing sales trends with the client.

Step 4: Examine monthly history information for a single account.

Based on actual-to-budget variations reported on the comparative income statement, you may want to gather additional history information regarding a particular account. In the following steps, you examine the history of the Sales account.

1 Select **Inquiry >> Financial >> History Summary**.

2 Select account **000-4100-00**.

3 Select **2001** in the Year box to display the History Summary Inquiry window in Figure 1.4.

4 Select **File >> Print** to print the Inquiry window.

Unlike the Budget vs Actual window, the History Summary window does not provide a actual-to-history comparison. However, the window does provide useful information about the prior year's monthly account activity.

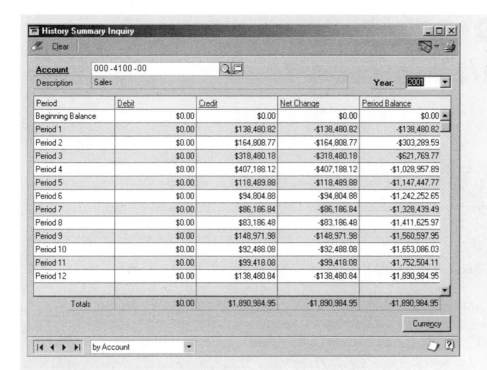

FIGURE 1.4

*History Summary
Inquiry Window*

Questions

1 Prepare the comparative income statement as of August 31, 2002, with actual-to-budget and actual-to-history analysis.

    a Print the income statement. Include a heading that contains the (1) company name, (2) statement description, and (3) date. Format the spreadsheet to project a professional image.

    b What is the actual-to-budget variance percent for Sales?

    c Identify the three accounts ($5,000 minimum balance) having the greatest actual-to-history variance percent. (Exclude summary items, such as Gross Profit on Sales.)

2 What was the actual-to-budget variance percent for Cost of Goods Sold in Periods 7 and 8?

3 Print the Budget vs Actual Inquiry window for Cost of Goods Sold.

4 What was the actual amount of Cost of Goods Sold in Periods 7 and 8 of 2001?

5 Print the History Summary Inquiry window for Cost of Goods Sold.

Project #2
Confirmation of Accounts Receivable

AUDIT OBJECTIVE

Determine the existence of individual accounts comprising accounts receivable.

STANDARD AUDIT PROCEDURE

Auditors will confirm a sample of accounts receivable if the total accounts outstanding is material to the financial statements. An auditor may select the confirmation sample using a variety of sampling techniques, depending on the perceived level of audit risk.

GATHERING EVIDENCE WITH DYNAMICS

Step 1: Obtain account information and outstanding balances.

Dynamics contains a routine that prints monthly customer statements and stores the value of the customer's outstanding balance. This balance is available to Explorer, enabling you to create a list of all customers and their outstanding balances. Because SLI's customers are located within a small geographic area, you can confirm accounts receivable at year end.

1 Modify the user date to **12/31/2002**.

2 Select **Explorer >> Customers >> Default**.

3 Click **Columns** to remove the following columns: **Address 2**, **Phone 1**.

4 Add the following column: **Last Statement Amount, Last Statement Date**.

5 Click **Search** to enter the criteria **Customer Number is not equal to 9999**. Click **OK** to save.
   SLI's account 9999 is the point-of-sale system. The account should not be selected for confirmation.

6 Click **Favorites** to save the view as **Audit Confirmation**.

7 Export the data to **Excel**.

Step 2: Reconcile the search results to the general ledger account.

Before selecting a sample, you must ensure that the search results represent a complete list of the outstanding accounts receivable. The sum of the individual accounts should be compared to the amount reported in the general ledger.

1 In Excel, use a SUM function to calculate the total of the accounts.

2 In Dynamics, select **Inquiry >> Financial >> Summary**.

3 Select account **000-1200-00** to view the Summary Inquiry window for Accounts Receivable.

Any material difference between the search results total and the general ledger should be reconciled by client personnel. You must then decide if any of the reconciling items should alter the accounts or amounts from which the sample will be selected.

Step 3: Select a sample of accounts and send positive confirmations.

Auditors may use a variety of sampling techniques to select the sample of confirmations to be sent to customers. This project illustrates how an Excel tool can be used to select a random sample.

1 In Excel, select **Tools >> Data Analysis**.

If, when you select Tools, you do not see Data Analysis as an option, then do the following:

*1. Select **Tools>>Add-Ins**.*

*2. In the Add-Ins list that appears, select the Analysis ToolPak box, then click **OK**.*

Now, when you return to the Tools menu, Data Analysis should appear as an option.

2 Select **Sampling** to open the Sampling window shown in Figure 2.1.

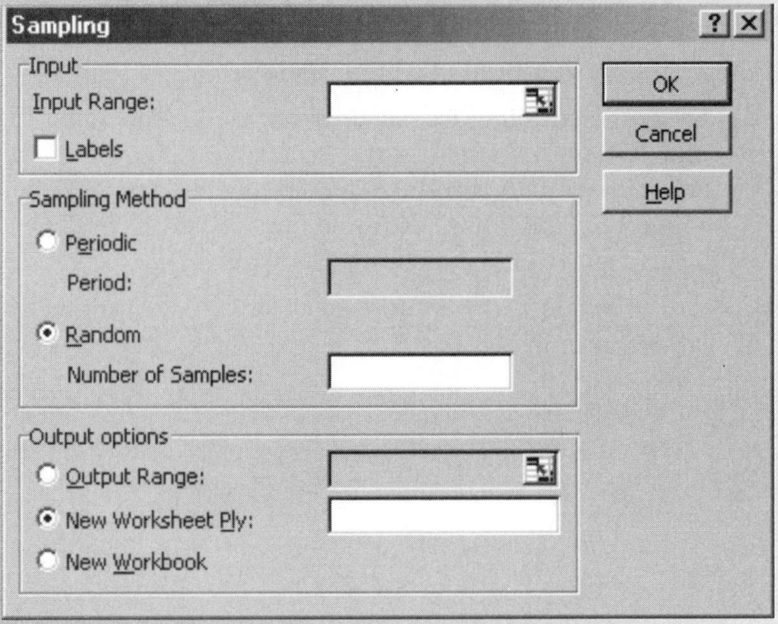

FIGURE 2.1
Excel Sampling Window

> The sampling technique selected for this project may result in an account being selected more than once. Thus, an auditor wanting to confirm 12 accounts would select a sample number greater than 12. If more than 12 unique accounts are selected, the auditor would simply confirm the first 12 accounts selected.

FYI

FYI

🔲 *Minimize*

🔳 *Maximize*

Clicking the Minimize button minimizes the window and returns your control to the worksheet, enabling you to highlight the desired range of cells. To return to the window, click the Maximize button on the minimized window.

3 Click **Minimize** in the Input Range box to minimize the dialog box.

4 Highlight the account numbers in column A, including the column heading.

5 Click **Maximize** to view the Sampling window.

6 Click the **Labels** check box.

7 Make sure the **Random** radio button is filled.

8 Enter **20** in the Number of Samples box.

9 Click on the **Output Range** radio button.

10 Click **Minimize** in the Output Range box and select cell A1 of Sheet2.

11 Click **Maximize**.

12 Click **OK**.

Sheet2 now contains a list of customer account numbers. Excel's Advanced Filter tool can be used to create a list of the accounts to be confirmed. First, the list on Sheet2 will be modified to serve as the criteria range for the filter. The filter will then prepare a list of accounts on Sheet3.

13 Insert a row at row 1 of Sheet2.

14 Copy the column heading at Sheet1!A1, Customer Number, to Sheet2!A1.

15 Select **Sheet3**.
The output of the filter must be on the active sheet. Thus, it is best to begin entering these commands on a blank sheet.

16 Select **Data >> Filter >> Advanced Filter**.

17 Select the **Copy to another location** radio button.

18 Using the Minimize and Maximize buttons:

   a Select the customer information on Sheet1, including the column headings, in the List range box.

   b Select the list of account numbers on Sheet2, including the column heading, in the Criteria range box

   c Select cell A1 of Sheet3 in the Copy to box.

19 Click the **Unique records only** check box. Your window should appear as shown in Figure 2.2.

20 Click **OK**. The list of accounts to be confirmed is created on Sheet3.

21 Save the spreadsheet as **Confirmations**.

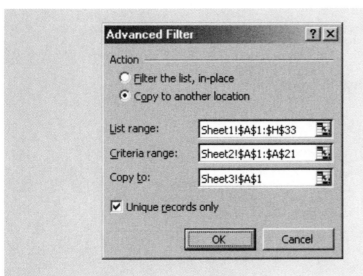

FIGURE 2.2

Excel Advanced Filter WIndow

The Confirmations worksheet can also be used for an analysis of the confirmation results. Auditors typically classify confirmation responses into several categories, including confirmed correct, confirmed with exception, unable to reply, and no reply.

FYI

Step 4: Prepare the confirmation letters.

The final step to prepare the confirmation letters is to merge the filtered list of customer accounts with the confirmation letter. Word contains a Mail Merge Helper to guide you through the process. The confirmation letter has already been prepared for you.

1 In Word, open the file **Confirmation Letter**.

2 Select **Tools >> Mail Merge >> Options** to open the Mail Merge Helper window.

3 In step 1, select **Create >> Form Letters**.

4 In step 2, select **Get Data >> Open Data Source**.

5 Select **MS Excel Worksheets** in the Files of type box.

6 Select the **Confirmations** file and click **Open**.

7 Select **Entire Spreadsheet** and click **OK**. Your window should now appear as shown in Figure 2.3.

8 In step 3, select **Merge**.

9 Select **Merge** in the Merge window. Word creates a new document that contains a page for each account confirmed.

The coding within the Word document, such as <<Customer_Name>> correlates with the column headings in the Excel spreadsheet.

FYI

> January 5, 2003
>
> <<Customer_Name>>
> <<Address_1>>
> <<City>>, <<State>>, <<Zip>>
>
> We would appreciate your assistance in providing our independent accountants, Smith & Smith, LLC, with an independent confirmation of your receivable balance with us.

FIGURE 2.3

Word Mail Merge Helper Window

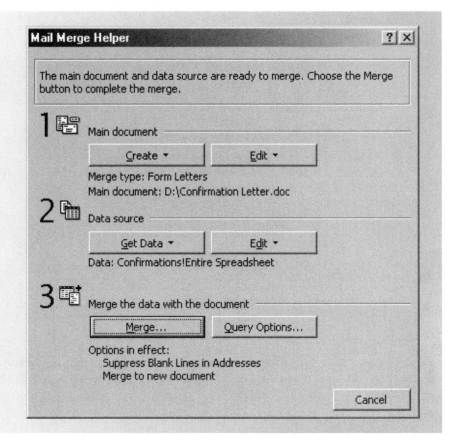

Questions

1 Identify the total amount of the accounts according to (1) the Explorer search results and (2) the 12/31/2002 Accounts Receivable balance in the general ledger. How will the difference impact the confirmation process?

2 From the requested sample of 20 accounts, how many unique accounts were selected?

3 Print the first page of Sheet3 from the Confirmations spreadsheet. (*Note:* Do *not* enter any heading information on this spreadsheet as it will disrupt the mail merge process.)

4 Print the form letter Confirmation Letter.

5 Print the first three confirmation letters.

Project #3
Physical Inventory Observation

AUDIT OBJECTIVE

Determine that the client's count of items in inventory is accurate and complete.

STANDARD AUDIT PROCEDURE

Auditors observe the client's year-end physical inventory and perform random test counts for subsequent comparison to the priced inventory. The test counts should include high-cost inventory.

GATHERING EVIDENCE WITH DYNAMICS

Step 1: Obtain quantity and cost information for all inventory items.

Explorer can create a list of inventory items sorted in descending order by value. You should create this list as close to the fiscal year end as possible.

1 Select **Explorer >> Item Quantities >> Default**.

2 Click **Columns** to remove the following columns: **Record Type**, **QTY on Order**, **QTY Allocated**, **QTY Available**.

3 Add the **Current Cost** column.

4 Click **Search** to enter the criteria **Location Code is equal to COLUMBUS**.

5 **Sort** the search results in descending order by Current Cost.

6 Click **Favorites** to save the view as **Audit Physical Inventory**.

7 Export the data to **Excel**.

Step 2: Reconcile the search results to the general ledger account.

Before selecting a sample, the auditor should gain some level of assurance that the Explorer search results represent a complete list of the outstanding inventory. The sum of the total current costs provides an approximate value of the inventory that can be compared to the amount reported in the general ledger.

1 In Excel, add a column containing formulas to calculate the total cost of each item. Label the column **Total Cost**.

2 Use a SUM function to calculate the total of the Total Cost column.

3 In Dynamics, select **Inquiry >> Financial >> Summary**.

4 Select account **000-1300-00** to view the Summary Inquiry for Inventory.

5 Compare the total cost calculated on the Excel spreadsheet with the recorded amount in the general ledger.

The two inventory cost totals will differ since one is calculated using current costs while the other uses the FIFO method. In periods of rising costs, a total calculated using current costs should be higher. Based on your knowledge of the client, you will be able to assess whether the difference is a result of the different costing methods. Any unexpected material difference between the search results total and the general ledger should be investigated by client personnel.

Step 3: Identify the inventory items with the highest cost.

Excel's filter tool can be used to select the items having the highest total cost.

1 Select **Data >> Filter >> AutoFilter**. Drop-down arrows will appear at the top of each column, as shown in Figure 3.1.

FIGURE 3.1

Excel AutoFilter

	A	B	C	D	E	F	G	H
1	Item Numb ▼	Location Co ▼	QTY On Ha ▼	Item Description ▼	Current Co ▼	Total Cost ▼		
2	999-9999	COLUMBUS	3	Portable Building	$4,599.99	$13,799.97		
3	632-4966	COLUMBUS	28	AntiParasitic	$249.60	$6,988.80		
4	104-6309	COLUMBUS	30	Sprayer	$115.99	$3,479.70		
5	451-9704	COLUMBUS	1	Crepe Myrtle -- 30 gal	$112.17	$112.17		

2 Click on the **AutoFilter** arrow in the Total Cost column.

3 Select **(Top 10....)** to view the Top 10 AutoFilter window in Figure 3.2.

FIGURE 3.2

Excel Top 10 AutoFilter Window

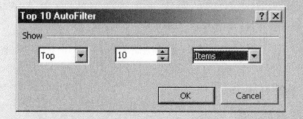

4 Change the number of items selected from 10 to

5 Save the spreadsheet as **Physical Inventory**.

You now have a list of items that should be included in your inventory test counts.

Questions

1 Identify the total amount of the inventory according to (1) the Explorer search results and (2) the 12/31/2002 inventory balance in the general ledger.

2 Print the following lists using the Physical Inventory spreadsheet. Include a heading containing the client name, report description, and date.

   a The 20 inventory items having the highest total cost.

   b Inventory items having no quantity on hand (change the Total Cost filter to All before selecting a new filter).

   c The 25 inventory items having the highest per unit cost.

3 Print a physical inventory count sheet reporting all the inventory items. Select **Reports >> Inventory >> Activity >> Stock Status**. Why might you print this report rather than performing the procedures illustrated in this project?

...unts

...their net realizable

...nts receivable be ... balance of the ...ible Accounts, ...ring the next

...s of management's adjustment ...e the aging of accounts receivable. Two ...d to estimate the adjustment: (1) applying a per- ...gross or net sales, or (2) applying percentages to outstand- ...its in an aged trial balance. Regardless of the procedures used to ...imate the allowance adjustment, the auditor should inquire about accounts that are significantly overdue. If appropriate, the auditor should recommend that management write off these accounts.

GATHERING EVIDENCE WITH DYNAMICS

Step 1: Determine the accuracy of the adjustment calculation.

SLI records a monthly adjustment to the allowance account equal to 2.5 percent of credit sales. Except for sales generated by the point-of-sale system (account 9999), all sales are credit sales. Thus, calculating credit sales requires subtracting the point-of-sale system sales from total sales. In the following steps, you will examine the adjustment for September.

1. Select **Inquiry >> Financial >> Summary**.
2. Select account **000-4100-00**.
3. Record sales for September as displayed in the Net Change column.
4. Close all open windows and palettes.
5. Select **Inquiry >> Sales >> Period Summary**.

6 Enter account **9999**.

7 Select **9** in the Period/Month box.

8 Record September sales for the point-of-sale system.

9 Using a calculator, calculate total credit sales and the adjustment to the allowance account.

The Summary Inquiry window denotes credit amounts in the Net Change and Period Balance columns with a negative sign.

FYI

Step 2: Determine that the allowance adjustment is recorded in the accounting system.

The allowance adjustment is entered using a journal entry. Use Dynamics to examine the amount and account distribution of the adjustment. The adjustment can be located by examining the detail of the Bad Debt expense account. You can then zoom on the transaction to examine its detail.

1 Select **Inquiry >> Financial >> Detail**.

2 Select the **Bad Debts** account.

3 Identify the September adjustment.

4 Select **File >> Print** to print the window.

5 Highlight the 9/30/02 adjustment and click **Journal Entry** to examine the transaction details. You may have to use the scroll bar to view the debit portion of the transaction.

6 Click **Show** to view the account distribution.

Step 3: Identify any outstanding receivables that should be written off.

An aged trial balance is one method auditors use to identify outstanding accounts that should be written off. Use Dynamics to prepare the aging of accounts receivable.

1 Select **Reports >> Sales >> Trial Balance**.

2 Select **Aged Trial Balance w/Options** in the Reports box.

3 Click **New** to create a new report.

4 Name the option **Audit Aging Schedule**.

5 Click the **In Detail** check box to remove the check (to view a summary report).

6 Select all customers.

7 Click **Insert** to enter the Customer ID information in the Restrictions box.

FYI

Always print a report to screen first. Once you determine that the report provides the information you need, change the destination to prepare a printed copy of the report.

8 Click **Destination** and change the report destination to screen only.

9 Click **OK** and **Print** to view the report on the screen.

10 After viewing the report, modify the destination to print pages the report.

11 **Save** the report format.

The client's efforts to collect an account should be recorded in Dynamics. The client can also place a hold on the account to prevent additional sales to the customer. Having used the aged trial balance to identify customers having outstanding accounts, use Dynamics to review these collection efforts. The following steps show you how to review the account for J & J Farms.

12 Select **Cards >> Sales >> Customer**.

13 Select **1001** in the Customer ID box.

14 Examine the Comment 1 and Comment 2 boxes for evidence of collection activity.

15 Examine the attached note.

16 Determine if the customer account has been placed on hold (the Hold check box would be checked).

Examining individual sales transactions may also identify reasons for customer non-payment. Use Dynamics to examine detailed information for the outstanding invoices of customers having overdue accounts. Follow these steps to examine the sales transactions for PWC Farming, Inc.

17 Select **Inquiry >> Sales >> Trx by Customer**.

18 Select **1111** in the Customer ID box.

19 Click **Show** to reveal the Amount Remaining amount.

20 Highlight **INV0125** and click **Document Number**.

21 Examine the attached note.

Having gathered all the evidence available in Dynamics, you should now discuss this information with client personnel. Only then can you make decisions as to whether an account can be collected.

Questions

1 Determine the amount of October credit sales.

2 Print the Detail Inquiry window for the Bad Debt account.

3 Determine the reasonableness of the total adjustment to the allowance account. *Hint:* Select **Inquiry >> Sales >> Yearly Summary** to identify annual sales for the point-of-sale system.

4 Print the aged trial balance as of 12/31/2002.

5 What is the total amount of accounts 91 and Over days past due as of 12/31/2002?

6 For each customer having a 91 and Over days past due account greater than $2,500:

    a Determine if the account has been put on hold.

    b Determine if any evidence suggests that the account should be written off. Support your answer with information collected from comment boxes and notes.

Project #5

Obsolete Inventory

Determine that inventory is priced at the lower of cost or market.

STANDARD AUDIT PROCEDURE

Generally accepted accounting principles require that inventory be reported at the lower of cost or market. Inventory items may become obsolete as a result of several factors, such as technological advances or changes in consumer preferences. Calculating an inventory turnover for each item can reveal items whose quantity on hand is excessive. A low inventory turnover ratio is an indication that an item is not selling quickly relative to the quantity of the item in inventory.

GATHERING EVIDENCE WITH DYNAMICS

Step 1: Obtain the information required to calculate an inventory turnover.

Explorer can create a list of inventory items that includes the two items required to calculate the inventory turnover ratio: quantity on hand and quantity sold.

1 Select **Explorer >> Item Quantities >> Default**.

2 Click **Columns** to remove the following columns: **Record Type, QTY On Order, QTY Allocated, QTY Available**.

3 Add the **QTY Sold** column.

4 Click **Search** to enter the criteria **Location Code is equal to Columbus**.

5 Click **Favorites** to save the view as **Audit Obsolete**.

6 Export the search results to **Excel**.

Step 2: Calculate the inventory turnover.

The inventory turnover is calculated by dividing the quantity sold by the quantity on hand. This calculation can be created in Excel and the inventory list sorted to highlight those inventory items with the lowest turnover ratio.

1 In Excel, enter the column heading **Inventory Turnover** in the next available column. Adjust the column width or format the cell with wrap alignment to properly view the heading.

2 Enter a formula to calculate the inventory turnover for each item. Display the values in an appropriate format.

Having calculated the inventory turnover ratio, you can sort the list to highlight the items having the lowest turnover ratio.

3 Position the cell pointer on any cell within the list.

4 Select **Data >> Sort** to open a Sort window similar to Figure 5.1.

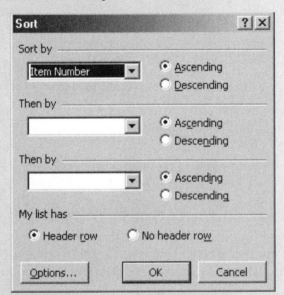

*To wrap text in an Excel cell, select **Format>>Cells>> Alignment.** Click on the Wrap text check box. The column height should automatically adjust to enable the label to be displayed on multiple rows.*

FIGURE 5.1
Excel Sort Window

Excel uses the term list to refer to a table of data. Because Excel uses the column headings to identify each data item in the list, these headings should be unique. Positioning the cell pointer within the list when selecting the Sort tool enables Excel to identify the cells that comprise the list.

FYI

FYI

5 Select **Inventory Turnover** in the Sort by box.

6 Select **Ascending** order.

7 Ensure that the **Header row** radio button is selected.

8 Click **OK**.

9 Save the spreadsheet as **SLI Obsolete Inventory**.

The slowest-moving inventory items are displayed at the top of the list. After printing a portion of the list, you can begin the process obtaining additional evidence.

Step 3: Investigate the slowest moving items.

The inventory turnover ratio provides insight regarding sales activity for an entire fiscal year. Before discussing any inventory item with your client, gaining additional information, such as monthly unit sales, will be useful to assess whether an item should be classified as obsolete.

If the company has selected the Dynamics' inventory history option, a monthly history of unit sales is available. SLI selected this option for all items in March. The following steps show you how to examine the monthly history for item 701-3311.

1 In Dynamics, select **Cards >> Inventory >> History**.

2 Select item **701-3311**.

3 Examine the Sales Quantity column to identify any trend in sales that might provide insight into whether the item is obsolete.

Questions

1 Analyze the unit sales activity for the ten items having the lowest inventory turnover as calculated on the SLI Obsolete Inventory spreadsheet.

   a Classify each item in one of the following categories. Record your conclusion in a column labeled "Evaluation."

      i. Obsolete—Unit sales are declining; the current inventory will not be sold within the next fiscal year.

      ii. Overstock—Unit sales are steady; SLI appears to have over-purchased. Sale of the remaining stock appears likely within the next fiscal year.

      iii. Seasonal—Unit sales are seasonal, resulting in a misleading inventory turnover ratio.

   b Examine the sales history for each item. Add a column to the spreadsheet containing a brief analysis of each item. Label the column **Comment**. Format the column using the wrap text option.

2 Print the first page of an inventory turnover report using a report format provided in Dynamics. Select **Reports >> Inventory >> Analysis >> Turnover Report**.

   a Print the report containing all the inventory items.

   b Describe how the inventory turnover is calculated on this report.

   c Why would an auditor print this inventory turnover report rather than use Explorer to export similar data for analysis in Excel?

Project #6

Inventory Costing

Determine the appropriate FIFO layers were used to cost the year-end inventory.

STANDARD AUDIT PROCEDURE

The auditor should select a sample of inventory items to verify the unit costs used to value the ending inventory.

GATHERING EVIDENCE WITH DYNAMICS

Step 1: Prepare a report containing the inventory layers.

SLI uses FIFO to value its inventory. Thus, the unit costs used to price the ending inventory consist of the most recent purchases. Dynamics has a report format that shows all inventory receipts and which items are considered to be sold. The report also shows the total FIFO value of inventory.

1 Select **Reports >> Inventory >> Activity**.

2 Select the **Purchase Receipts** report.

3 Click **New** to create a new report format.

4 Enter the option name **Audit Inventory Costing**.

5 Select **Qty Type** in the Ranges box.

6 Select **On Hand** in the From and To boxes.

7 Click **Insert** to enter the segment information in the Restrictions box.

8 Click **Destination** and change the report destination to the screen only.

9 Click **OK** and **Print** to view the report on the screen.

10 After viewing the report, modify the report destination to print on a printer.

11 Print the first and last two pages of the report.

The Purchase Receipts report shows the source of the inventory items, and thus the layers used to value the ending inventory. Examine the header section to identify the items presented on the report. The quantity on hand for any inventory item can be calculated by subtracting the Quantity Sold from the Quantity Received.

Step 2: Reconcile the total remaining value to the general ledger account.

Before selecting a sample, the auditor must ensure that the report represents a complete list of the inventory and layers. The total value remaining should equal the account balance of Inventory in the general ledger.

1 Select **Inquiry >> Financial >> Summary**.

2 Select account **000-1300-00** to view the Summary Inquiry window.

3 Compare the Period 12 balance to the total of the Purchase Receipts report.

Any material difference between the Purchase Receipts report total and general ledger balance should be reconciled by client personnel. The nature and amount of the reconciling items will determine if you propose an adjustment to inventory.

Step 3: Compare the quantity on hand to the inventory records.

The quantity on hand, as calculated from the report, should match the quantity on hand in the inventory records. You may elect to make this comparison for a sample of inventory items.

1 Select **Cards >> Inventory >> Item**.

2 Select item **104-6300**.

3 Compare the quantity on hand per the Purchase Receipts report to the quantity on hand shown on the Item Maintenance window.

Step 4: Examine the transaction detail for selected inventory receipts.

The unit cost used to price the inventory should be compared to the original transaction. As with your testing of the quantities on hand, you may elect to make this comparison for a sample of inventory items. The following steps show how to examine transactions for item 104-6300.

1 Select **Inquiry >> Inventory >> Receipts**.

2 Select item **104-6300**.

3 Select **Columbus** in the Site ID box.

4 Click **Show** to display the document numbers.

5 Select **RCT0009**.

6 Compare the quantity and unit cost with the values on the Purchase Receipts report.

Some receipts reported on the Purchase Receipts report result from sales returns. These transactions can also be examined using the Purchase Inquiry Receipts window.

7 Select **INV0171**.

8 Click **Receipt Number** to view the transaction detail.

9 Click **Distributions** to determine how this transaction was recorded in the general ledger.

A returned item that is salable is returned to the inventory, resulting in a debit entry to Inventory. Damaged inventory is thrown away, resulting in a debit entry to 000-4520-00, Cost of Goods Sold—Shrinkage.

Questions

1 Print the first and last two pages of the Purchase Receipts report as of 12/31/2002.

2 Examine the unit costs assigned to item 999-0031, Flag. How did Dynamics assign the FIFO layers to the units on hand?

3 The unit cost of item 104-6309, Sprayer, increased from $111.73 to $115.99. Did Dynamics use the correct unit cost in assigning a value to the ending inventory?

4 Identify the difference between the inventory total according to the Purchase Receipts report and the general ledger balance as of 12/31/2002.

5 For inventory items 104-6300 and 999-9999, identify the
   a quantity on hand on the Purchase Receipts report.
   b quantity on hand in the inventory records.
   c receipt number of the last receipt (excluding sales returns).
   d unit cost on the last receipt.
   e vendor doc. no. of the last receipt.

Project #7

Inventory Shrinkage Reserve

AUDIT OBJECTIVE

Evaluate the reasonableness of the monthly adjustment for inventory shrinkage.

STANDARD AUDIT PROCEDURE

Inventory can shrink for a variety of reasons, including internal theft, shoplifting, and damage. Generally accepted auditing standards require that companies having a material amount of inventory perform an annual physical inventory to quantify the amount of shrinkage. Most companies perform this task near their fiscal year end.

Rather than waiting until year end to reflect the cost of shrinkage in the financial statements, retail businesses can record monthly estimates of the shrinkage to an inventory contra account. The auditor should examine the assumptions used in the estimate to assess the validity of the assumptions and the accuracy of the calculations.

GATHERING EVIDENCE WITH DYNAMICS

Step 1: Evaluate the monthly shrinkage adjustment.

SLI estimates inventory shrinkage as 1 percent of the monthly cost of goods sold. An adjustment is made to Inventory Shrinkage Reserve, an inventory contra account, and Cost of Goods Sold-Shrinkage. Evaluating a monthly adjustment involves identifying cost of goods sold for a month, calculating the adjustment, then tracing the amount to the adjusting entry. In the following steps, you will verify the accuracy of the June adjustment.

1 Select **Inquiry >> Financial >> Summary**.

2 Select the **Cost of Goods Sold** account.

3 Identify June's cost of goods sold by examining the Net Change column.

4 Calculate the shrinkage adjustment for June.
Use a calculator, if necessary.

5 Select the **Cost of Goods Sold—Shrinkage** account.

6 Highlight **Period 6** (June) and click any of the zoom features.

7 Click **Journal Entry** to examine the journal entry.

Step 2: Evaluate the shrinkage assumption.

You can evaluate the year-end account balances of the Cost of Goods Sold and Cost of Goods Sold—Shrinkage accounts to assess the validity of the shrinkage rate assumption. Calculating the actual shrinkage as a percent of cost of goods sold will provide insight regarding the SLI's 1 percent shrinkage rate assumption.

1 Select **Inquiry >> Financial >> Summary**.

2 Select the **Cost of Goods Sold** account and record the last period balance.

3 Select the **Cost of Goods Sold—Shrinkage** account and record the last period balance.

4 Calculate the actual shrinkage rate.
Use a calculator, if necessary.

FYI

*To use the Window's calculator, select **Start>> Programs>>Accessories>> Calculator**.*

Step 3: Examine the inventory shrinkage adjustment for unusual items.

A difference (variance) between the perpetual and physical inventory counts, by itself, provides little information on how or why particular items experienced shrinkage. Calculating a ratio of the shrinkage relative to unit sales provides a clearer picture of the degree to which an inventory item is at risk. The ratio, identified here as the shrinkage ratio, requires that you compare the year-end inventory adjustment to annual unit sales for each item.

Calculating the shrinkage ratio requires several steps. First, separate Explorer searches are required to obtain the quantity adjustment and unit sales. After these lists are exported to Excel, a consolidation of the two spreadsheets is performed to create a single list. Finally, the ratio is calculated using the information on the consolidated spreadsheet.

Begin by identifying the journal entry used to record the adjustments. This information will be required to create an Explorer search.

1 Select **Inquiry >> Financial >> Detail**.

2 Select the **Inventory Shrinkage Reserve** account.

3 Enter **IVADJ** in the Source Document From box.
IVADJ is an abbreviation for Inventory Adjustment.

4 Click **Redisplay**.

5 Highlight any of the transactions and click **Journal Entry**.

6 Record the Batch ID number of the transaction.

Dynamics has an inventory transaction option designed specifically to record periodic counts of inventory. The option automatically creates a journal entry to adjust the inventory account. SLI used the option to record the actual inventory counts on 12/31/2002. The difference or variance was recorded to the Inventory Shrinkage Reserve account. The transactions you see on the Transaction Entry Zoom window are adjustments for the variance of each inventory item.

Explorer can be used to create a list of this transaction and export the list to Excel for further analysis.

7 Select **Explorer >> Inventory Transactions >> Default**.

8 Click **Columns** to remove the following columns: **U Of M**, **Document Status**, **Extended Cost**, **TRX Location**, **Document Date**.

9 Add the **TRX Source** column.

10 Click **Search** to enter the criteria **TRX Source is equal to** the Batch ID identified in step 6.
TRX is an abbreviation for Transaction.

11 Click **Favorites** to save the view as **Audit Inventory Adjustments**.

12 Export the search to **Excel**.

13 Save the spreadsheet as **SLI Inventory Adjustments**.

The inventory adjustment for each item should be compared to the quantity of the item sold. Use Explorer to prepare a list of unit sales by inventory item.

14 In Dynamics, select **Explorer >> Item Quantities >> Default**.

15 Click **Columns** to remove the following columns: **Record Type**, **QTY On Order**, **QTY Allocated**, **QTY Available**.

16 Add the **QTY Sold** column.

17 On the Change Column Display window, as shown in Figure 7.1, highlight the **QTY On Hand** column.

FIGURE 7.1

Explorer Change Column Display WIndows

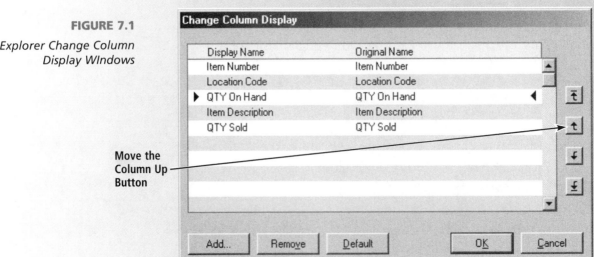

Move the Column Up Button

18 Click the **Move the column up** button to move the QTY On Hand to the second position.

19 Use the **Move the column up** button to move QTY Sold to the third position.

20 Click **Search** to enter the criteria **Location Code is equal to Columbus**.

21 Click **Favorites** to save the view as **Audit Unit Sales**.

22 Export the search to **Excel**.

23 Save the spreadsheet as **SLI Unit Sales**.

You now have the information required to calculate the shrinkage ratio. Unfortunately, the information is currently located on separate spreadsheets. You will have to consolidate the two spreadsheets together to calculate the ratio. Several techniques could be used to connect these two information sources. Excel's consolidation tool was selected for this project.

24 Open the **Inventory Adjustments** spreadsheet.

25 Select **Sheet2**.

26 Select **Data >> Consolidate** to open the consolidate window in Figure 7.2.

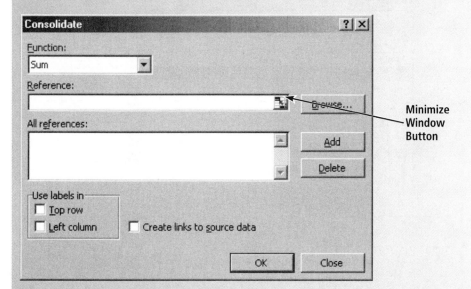

FIGURE 7.2

Excel Consolidate Window

Minimize Window Button

27 Click the **Minimize** button in the Reference box.

28 Select the **Item Number** and **TRX QTY** columns on Sheet1. Include the column headings on row 1.

29 Click the **Maximize** button on the minimized Consolidate—Reference window, as shown in Figure 7.3.

The data to be used in the Excel consolidation should be in adjacent columns. This task could also be performed in Excel.

FYI

FIGURE 7.3
Consolidate—Reference Window

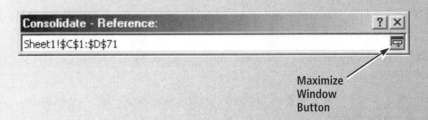

Maximize
Window
Button

Excel's consolidation tool uses the labels in the first row and left column of each reference. Cells having similar row and column labels are combined (consolidated). For this project, consolidation uses the labels in the Item Number, the first column in each reference, to bring the TRX QTY, Unit Cost, and QTY Sold together.

30 Click **Add** to record the reference in the All references box.

31 Click the **Minimize** button in the Reference box.

32 Select the **SLI Unit Sales** button on the Windows task bar.

33 Select the **Item Number**, **QTY On Hand**, and **QTY Sold** columns on Sheet1, including the column headings on row 1.

34 Click the **Maximize** button on the minimized Consolidate— Reference window.

35 Click **Add** to record the reference in the All references box.

36 Click the **Top row** and **Left column** check boxes. Your window should now appear similar to Figure 7.4.

FIGURE 7.4
Excel Consolidate Window

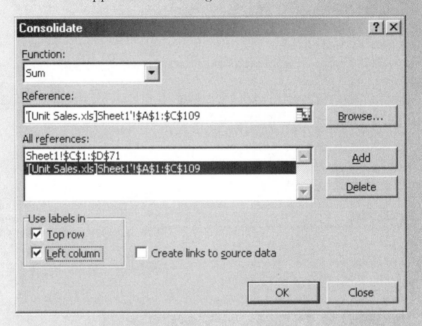

37 Click **OK** to view the consolidation.

Excel has consolidated the two data sources, combining the data for each inventory item. Inventory items having a blank in the TRX QTY column did not have a year-end variance adjustment. The TRX QTY and QTY Sold columns will be used in this analysis.

38 In Excel, create formulas to calculate the shrinkage ratio for each item (TRX QTY divided by QTY Sold). Format the amount using **percent,1** format.

39 Label the column **Shrinkage Ratio**.

40 Position the cell pointer on any cell in the list.

41 Select **Data >> Filter >> AutoFilter**. Drop-down arrows will appear at the top of each column, as shown in Figure 7.5.

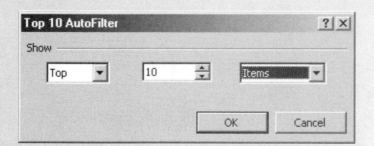

	A	B	C	D	E	F	G
		TRX QT ▼	QTY On Hand ▼	QTY So ▼	Shrinkage Ratio ▼		
1	▼						
2	104-6300	-1	178	386	-0.3%		
3	104-6309	-2	30	603	-0.3%		
4	113-2749	-1	163	1,596	-0.1%		

FIGURE 7.5
Excel AutoFilter

> Select **Format>>Cells>> Alignment>>Wrap text** to wrap text within a cell.

FYI

42 Click on the AutoFilter arrow in the **Shrinkage Ratio** column.

43 Select the **(Top 10….)** option to view the Top10 AutoFilter window in Figure 7.6.

FIGURE 7.6
Excel Top 10 AutoFilter Window

44 Change the number of items selected from 10 to **20**.

45 Since an inventory loss is recorded as a negative number in the TRX QTY column, change the order box from Top to **Bottom**.

46 Click **OK**.

47 Print the filtered list.

You now have a list of the inventory items that experienced the greatest rate of loss. Physical size, value, and other factors can influence the frequency of internal theft and shoplifting. Physical factors, such as erosion and evaporation, may naturally cause shrinkage. You are now prepared to talk with client personnel about potential inventory shrinkage problems.

Questions

1   What was the amount of the September inventory shrinkage adjustment? Was the amount calculated and recorded correctly?

2   What is SLI's actual inventory shrinkage rate for fiscal year 2002?

3   Identify the transaction number(s) of the year-end adjustment based on the physical inventory counts.

4   Print a report of the 25 inventory items having the highest shrinkage ratios. Insert a report heading that includes the client name, report description, and audit fiscal year.

5   What changes to the spreadsheet would improve the understandability of the report?

Project #8

Capital Leases

AUDIT OBJECTIVE

Determine that new leases have bee[n] [correctly recorded as cap]ital leases.

STANDARD AUDIT P[ROGRAM]

In accordance with SFAS 13 as amended, a lease th[at transfers] all the risks and benefits of ownership should be recorded as a cap[ital lease.] Searching rent expense accounts is one method an auditor can use to identify new rent payments and the related lease agreements.

GATHERING EVIDENCE WITH DYNAMICS

Step 1: Identify new lease payments.

SLI charges lease payments to Rent, account 000-5260-00. You can quickly detect a new rental agreement by examining a monthly summary of the account. Zooming on the transaction detail can provide information about new leases. In the following steps, collect information on a new lease payment in November.

1 Select **Inquiry >> Financial >> Summary**.

2 Select **000-5260-00**, Rent, in the Account box.

3 Examine the monthly debits to the account, noting the months where the monthly rent payments changed.

4 Highlight **Period 11** and click **Net Change** to view the transactions. Compare the transactions with the previous month's to determine which transaction is new.

5 Click **Journal Entry**, then **Source Document** to obtain detailed information regarding the lease payment.

6 Read the attached note to the Journal Entry.

After preparing a list of new lease payments, you would ask the client to provide copies of the lease agreements. Each lease could then be evaluated to determine if it should be recorded as a capital lease.

SFAS 13 identifies four criteria for evaluating whether a lease should be recorded as a capital lease. The monthly payment, interest rate, and lease period provide useful information for two of these criteria (75 percent of useful life, 90 percent of fair market value). The following steps illustrate how to collect lease data for an item leased in November.

1 Select **Cards >> Fixed Assets >> Lease**.

2 Select **242** in the Asset ID box.

3 Record the lease type, payment, interest rate, and end date for the asset.

4 Select **Cards >> Fixed Assets >> General**.

5 Enter **242** in the Asset ID box.

6 Record the acquisition date.

Questions

1 In what month(s) did SLI enter into a new lease agreement?

2 For each lease, identify the following items (if available):
  a asset ID
  b description
  c acquisition date
  d acquisition cost
  e lease type
  f payment
  g interest rate
  h end date

Project #9

Unrecorded Fixed Assets

AUDIT OBJECTIVE

Determine that acquisitions of fixed assets are capitalized.

STANDARD AUDIT PROCEDURE

A review of certain expense accounts can detect the purchase of fixed assets. Fixed asset purchases may be improperly charged to supplies expense. Repairs of existing fixed assets that extend the assets' useful life may be improperly recorded as maintenance expense. If a client can use items from its inventory to build or enhance a fixed asset, a review of inventory adjustments can also reveal items that should be capitalized.

GATHERING EVIDENCE WITH DYNAMICS

Step 1: Search supplies and repair expenses for fixed asset purchases.

Southern Landscape's accounting policies require that any expenditure for a fixed asset greater than $500 be capitalized and depreciated over its useful life. SLI charges all supply purchases as expenses, recording a year-end adjusting entry to reflect the actual quantity of supplies on hand. Reviewing the activity in the Supplies expense account can reveal fixed asset purchases.

1 Select **Explorer >> Account Transactions >> Default.**

2 Click **Search** to enter the following criteria:

   a Account Number is equal to 000-5270-00
   b Debit amount is greater than 500.00

3 Enter **1500** in the Maximum Records box.
   This search may take a several seconds—the computer is searching over 1,400 records.

4 Click **Favorites** to save the view as **Audit Purchases**.

5 Record the journal entry number of any transaction in the search results.

Having identified a supply purchase that exceeded the $500 limit, you should now gather additional information regarding this transaction.

6 Select **Inquiry >> Financial >> Journal Entry**.

7 Enter **1270** in the Journal Entry box and press the **Tab** key.

8 Click **Source Document** to view the transaction details.

9 Read any information recorded in the transaction note.

The procedure presented in these steps is identical for the examination of transactions in any general ledger account.

10 Follow steps 1–9 to examine transactions in Equipment Repairs and Maintenance, account **000-5220-00**.

Step 2: Search inventory for fixed asset additions.

SLI has certain inventory items that could be used to landscape its store and warehouse. If the items are expected to last more than a season, the items should be added to the cost basis of the land. Inventory items used in the business are deducted from inventory using an inventory adjustment. Since adjustments were used to establish the beginning inventory on 12/31/2001, this search will look for adjustments in fiscal year 2002.

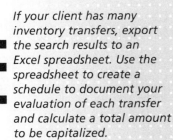

If your client has many inventory transfers, export the search results to an Excel spreadsheet. Use the spreadsheet to create a schedule to document your evaluation of each transfer and calculate a total amount to be capitalized.

1 Select **Explorer >> Inventory Transactions >> Default**.

2 Click **Search** to enter the following criteria:
   a Document Type is equal to Adjustment.
   b Document Date is greater than 12/31/01.

Planting annual flowers in its landscaping is a current expense for SLI since the flowers last only for a few months. However, planting bushes and trees should benefit the property for many years. Thus, you must examine the items transferred to determine if they constitute a current expense or capital expenditure. The following steps examine the first transaction in the search results.

3 Select any line of the first transaction in the search results.

4 Click **Go To**.

5 Select **Inventory Transaction Inquiry**.

6 Click **Show** to view descriptions for the items.

7 Read any information recorded in the transaction note.

8 Identify which items, if any, should be capitalized.
   Bushes, trees, and any material involved in their planting, such as top soil, should be capitalized if the items are added to existing capital assets.

9 Use a calculator or spreadsheet to determine the total cost of the items that qualify to for capitalization.

10 Close the Inventory Transaction Inquiry window to return to Explorer, allowing you to evaluate the remaining transactions.

Questions

1 Identify the supply purchases greater than $500. Write a statement that presents the information you have obtained and states your (1) next audit step or (2) conclusion.

2 Identify the repair and maintenance purchases greater than $500. Write a statement that presents the information you have obtained and states your (1) next audit step or (2) conclusion.

3 Identify any inventory adjustment greater than $500 (total value of all items). What amount, if any, should be capitalized? Write a statement that presents the information you have obtained and states your (1) next audit step or (2) conclusion.

Project #10

Depreciation Expense

AUDIT OBJECTIVE

Determine the reasonableness of depreciation expense.

STANDARD AUDIT PROCEDURE

Analytical analysis of depreciation expense accounts is the most cost effective audit procedure to gather evidence on the reasonableness of depreciation expense. The auditor can also examine a sample of acquired fixed assets to determine that the assigned depreciation method, useful life, and salvage values are appropriate.

GATHERING EVIDENCE WITH DYNAMICS

Step 1: Perform analytical analysis of depreciation expense.

The amount of depreciation recorded during the year can be compared to the budgeted amount. Several factors influence the monthly changes in depreciation, including (1) accelerated depreciation methods, (2) asset acquisitions, and (3) asset dispositions and retirements. You should evaluate the monthly depreciation amount relying on your knowledge of these factors.

1 Select **Inquiry >> Financial >> Budget vs. Actual**.
2 Select account **000-5110-00**, Depreciation.
3 Select **FY2002** in the Budget ID box.

Examine any period having a significant difference between the budget and actual amounts. The greatest difference involves periods 1 and 2. Use the Zoom feature to gather additional information on these periods.

4 Highlight **Period 2** and click **Actual**.
5 Highlight the transaction and click **Journal Entry** to view transaction details.
6 Read the information in the transaction note.

Examining the details of the transaction, including management's notes, can often provide you with the required audit evidence to make an informed decision.

Step 2: Examine the depreciation method assigned to fixed asset acquisitions.

When a fixed asset is purchased, SLI records the information in the fixed asset module. Using Explorer is the efficient method for preparing a list of new asset acquisitions.

1 Select **Explorer >> Fixed Assets >> Default**.

2 Click **Columns** to remove the following columns: **Suf, Location ID**.

3 Click **Search** to enter the criteria **Acquisition Date is greater than 12/31/2001**.

4 Click **Favorites** to save the view as **Audit Acquisitions**.

5 Print the search results.

An important part of recording an acquired fixed asset is assigning the depreciation method. The depreciation method for any fixed asset is determined by two factors:

Asset ID. Fixed assets are typically recorded in separate accounts, such as buildings and equipment, in the general ledger. The Asset ID enables a company to further categorize its assets to support different depreciation methods. The rapid technological obsolescence of computer equipment, for example, demands that its useful life be shorter than that of other office equipment. An Asset ID identifies the depreciation method, useful life, averaging convention, and switchover method for a similar group of fixed assets.

Book ID. Most companies report financial activity using a variety of accounting rules. GAAP is required for financial reporting. The Internal Revenue Code is required for tax reporting. Dynamics can depreciate assets using both GAAP and tax depreciation methods. A Book ID, such as Corporate or Federal, stores the applicable depreciation methods. SLI's corporate book ID calculates depreciation in accordance with GAAP.

To gain more insight into these factors, examine the windows used to set up the Asset ID and Book ID. In the following steps, you will examine the information related to asset 149.

6 Select **Inquiry >> Fixed Assets >> General**.

7 Select **149** in the Asset ID box.

8 Click **Class ID** to view the Class Setup window.

9 Click the **Lookup** button for Class ID to view the Class Setup Lookup window in Figure 10.1.

SLI has established eight asset classes, each having different depreciation method. Although several classes may use the straight-line depreciation method, for example, each class may use a different useful life.

FIGURE 10.1

Class Setup Lookup Window

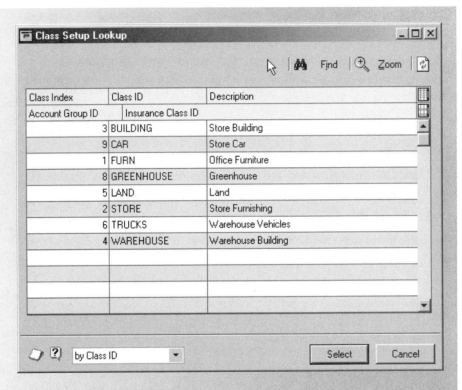

The Book Class Setup window in Figure 10.2 can be accessed only through the Setup menu option. For security reasons, SLI does not give its auditors access to this menu option. The window shows how buildings are depreciated for purposes of preparing GAAP financial statements.

FIGURE 10.2

Book Class Setup Window

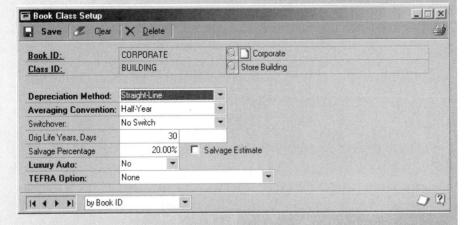

Armed with this knowledge of how depreciation methods are assigned, you can determine if the correct depreciation method was assigned to the fixed assets acquired during the fiscal year. In the following steps, you will examine the setup of the first asset on the search results.

10 Select **Inquiry >> Fixed Assets >> General**.

11 Enter **236** in the Asset ID box.

12 Determine the appropriateness of the assigned Class ID by referencing the list of Class ID in Figure 10.1.

Another Dynamics window provides similar info

13 Select **Cards >> Fixed Assets >> Book**.

14 Enter **236** in the Asset ID box.

15 Select **Corporate** in the Book ID to view the Asset Book w
Figure 10.3.

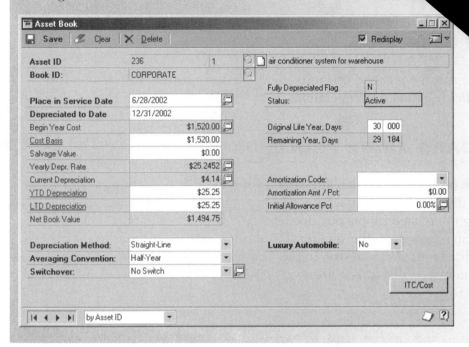

You can examine many aspects of the fixed asset using the Asset Book window, including the depreciation method, averaging convention, switchover method, and useful life.

Questions

1 Prepare a statement that presents the information you obtained regarding the February recording of depreciation expense.

2 What is the budget and actual depreciation expense for July?

3 Print a list of fixed assets acquired during fiscal year 2002. The list should contain the client's name, a description of the report, and the audit fiscal year.

4 Identify the following items for the assets acquired during fiscal year 2002:

    a asset ID

    b description

    c place in service date

    d cost basis

    e depreciation method

    f averaging convention

    g switchover method

    h useful life

mation.

window in

FIGURE 10.3
Asset Book Window

Depreciation Expense

Project 10

65

...ities

...ble balance includes all outstand-

...DURE

...e auditor examines accounts payable
...ubsequent to the audit year end. By
...umentation, such as shipping notices,
... can ensure that the transaction was
... addition, the auditor should determine
... year end are paid within a reasonable
period.

GATHERING EVIDENCE WITH DYNAMICS

Step 1: Identify invoices recorded subsequent to the fiscal year end.

Liabilities recorded in the Accounts Payable account subsequent to the audit year end should be examined to determine if they should have been recorded during the audit fiscal year. Use Dynamics to identify material transactions subsequent to the fiscal year end. Assume that materiality for this audit procedure is set at $10,000.

1 Select **Explorer >> Payables Transactions**.

2 Select **Columns** to remove **Current Trx Amount**.

3 Add the **Document Amount** column.

4 Select **Search** to enter the following criteria:
   a **Document Amount is greater than 9999**
   b **Document Type is equal to Invoice**
   c **Document Date is greater than 12312002**

5 Click **Favorites** to save the view as **Audit Payables Search**.

You now have a list of transactions to investigate. In addition to examining any source documents and obtaining inquiry evidence from client personnel, you may elect to examine detailed information for a transaction. If the number of transactions listed is relatively small, you can efficiently access the inquiry window directly from Explorer.

6   Select the first transaction on the search results.

7   Click **Go To**.

8   Select **Payables Transaction Entry Zoom**.

9   View any transaction notes.

10   Click the **Distributions** and **Apply** buttons to view detailed information regarding the transaction.

Step 2: Identify cash disbursements recorded subsequent to the fiscal year end.

Cash disbursements recorded subsequent to the audit year end should be examined to determine if the transactions should have been recorded in the audit fiscal year. Use Dynamics to identify material cash disbursements during the period after the fiscal year end. Assume that materiality for this audit procedure is set at $10,000.

1   Select **Explorer >> Bank Transactions**.

2   Select **Columns** to remove the **Description** column.

3   Add the **Paid ToRcvd From** column.
Paid ToRcvd From is an abbreviation for Paid To / Received From and contains the check payee name.

4   Select **Search** to enter the following criteria:
a   **Source Document is equal to PMPAY**
b   **Checkbook Amount is greater than 9999**
c   **GL Posting Date is greater than 12312002**
PMPAY is the audit trail code for Payment Entry

5   Click **Favorites** to save the view as **Audit Cash Payments**.

You now have a list of cash disbursements to investigate. Because the number of transactions listed is relatively small, accessing the inquiry windows directly from Explorer is an efficient procedure.

6   Select the first check on the search results.

7   Click **Go To**.

8   Select **Source Document**.

9   Click **Apply** to view the invoices paid by the check.

Step 3: Identify liabilities not paid subsequent to the fiscal year end.

An audit issue that relates closely to the search for unrecorded liabilities is a search for unpaid liabilities. A liability should be paid within a reasonable period after the year end. Use Dynamics to print an aged trial balance of accounts payable on a date during the year-end examination. Any unpaid invoice on the trial balance should be examined to determine if the liability really exists.

1 Select **Reports >> Purchasing >> Trial Balance**.

2 Select **Aged Trial Balance** in the Reports box.

3 Click **New** to create a new report option.

4 Name the report format **Audit Payables Aging**.

5 Enter **2/1/2003** in the Print/Age as of box.

6 Select all the vendors.

7 Click **Insert** to add all the vendors in the Restrictions box.

8 Click **Destination** and change the report destination to the screen only.

9 Click **OK** and **Print** to view the report on the screen.

10 After viewing the report, modify the destination to print the report to the printer.

11 **Save** the report option.

If the report is to contain all the items with no range, such as vendors, no range restriction needs to be entered.

You should examine any outstanding liability that is significantly past due. Spencer's American Gardening Equipment has several outstanding purchase invoices that remain unpaid.

12 Select **Inquiry >> Purchasing >> Trx by Vendor**.

13 Enter **104** in the Vendor ID box.

14 Click **Show** to reveal the second row of information for each transaction. The Unapplied Amount column shows the unpaid balance of each invoice.

15 Highlight voucher/payment number **238**.

16 Click **Document Number** to examine the transaction details.

17 Read any note attached to the transaction.

Questions

1 Identify information regarding invoice transactions equal to or greater than $10,000 recorded subsequent to 12/31/2002.

2 Identify information regarding cash disbursements equal to or greater than $10,000 recorded subsequent to 12/31/2002.

3 Print the aged Accounts Payable Trial Balance as of 2/1/2003.

4 For each outstanding invoice greater than $5000 reported on the Accounts Payable Trial Balance, collect the following information:

    a vendor ID

    b vendor name

    c receipt number

    d amount

    e invoice date

    f amount

    g evidence collected from document notes

Project #12

Vacation Accrual

AUDIT OBJECTIVE

Determine the reasonableness of the vacation accrual.

STANDARD AUDIT PROCEDURE

Unused vacation is a current liability. The amount should represent the wages that would be paid if all employees were paid in lieu of taking vacation time (an option often elected by employees upon their resignation). The auditor should verify the accuracy of the client's calculation of the vacation accrual, the sum of each employee's vacation time multiplied by the employee's wage rate.

GATHERING EVIDENCE WITH DYNAMICS

Step 1: Estimate the vacation accrual.

Dynamics accrues the number of days' vacation each employees has available. Each pay period the appropriate number of days' vacation is added to the employees' accounts. When an employee takes a vacation, the number of days is deducted from the employee's remaining vacation days.

SLI pays its employees on a semimonthly basis using an annual wage rate. Explorer can export the current vacation and recent payroll data to Excel by searching for transactions having a SAL (salary) payroll code.

1 Select **Explorer >> Payroll Historical Trx >> Default**.

2 Click **Columns** to remove the following columns: **Audit Control Code**, **UPR Trx Amount**.

3 Add the following columns: **Payroll Code**, **Check Date**, **Vacation Available**, **Pay Rate**.

4 Click **Search** to enter the criteria **Payroll Code is equal to SAL**.

5 Click **Sort** on the Check Date column.

6 Examine the search results to identify the last payroll date.

7 Click **Search** again and add the criteria **Check Date is equal to** to the date identified in the prior step.

8 Click **Favorites** to save the view as **Audit Vacation**.

9 Export the search results to **Excel**.

The search results contain the data required to make the vacation accrual calculation. You can use Excel to make these calculations.

10 In Excel, add a column to calculate the product of the Pay Rate and Vacation Available. Label the column **Vacation Accrual**.
Adjust the annual salary (pay rate) by 2080 hours to calculate a daily wage rate, then multiply the daily rate by the vacation (days) available.

11 Create a SUM function to calculate the sum of the Vacation Accrual column.

12 Save the spreadsheet as **SLI Vacation Accrual**.

Step 2: Compare the accrual estimate to the recorded value.

SLI does not attempt to maintain a monthly accrual of vacation expense. Instead, SLI makes one adjusting entry at the end of the year for purposes of preparing the annual financial statements. The accrual was recorded to the Salaries Payable account.

1 Select **Inquiry >> Financial >> Detail**.

2 Select account **000-2110-00**, Salaries Payable.

3 Select the 12/31/2002 adjustment and click **Journal Entry** to examine the transaction detail.

4 Read the attached note.

Step 3: Examine vacation information for a single employee.

Before concluding whether the vacation accrual is reasonable, you may elect to examine the vacation history and current information for a single employee. The following steps guide you through obtaining the current vacation information for John Patrick.

1 Select **Cards >> Payroll >> Employee**.

2 Select employee **01**, John Patrick, in the Employee ID box.

3 Click **Vac/Sick** to view the Employee Vacation-Sick Time Maintenance.

4 Note the number of vacation hours John Patrick receives each year and the number of hours available. Ensure that the available hours match the amount used for the vacation accrual.

The following steps enable you to examine John Patrick's vacation history.

5 Select **Inquiry >> Payroll >> Employee Pay History**.

6 Select employee **01**, John Patrick, in the Employee ID box.

7 Select **VAC** in the Pay Code box. The hours of vacation time taken appears in the Hours column.

You should examine how employees took their vacation time. Good internal control suggests that employees in control and cash handling positions be required to take extended vacations.

Questions

1 Print the SLI Vacation Accrual spreadsheet. Include a heading that contains the client name, document description, and audit fiscal year.

2 Identify the number, date, and amount of the vacation accrual adjusting entry.

3 Examine the current and historical vacation information for each employee. Identify any information that you conclude requires further investigation.

Project #13
Analytical Analysis of Sales

AUDIT OBJECTIVE

Determine that sales are fairly stated.

STANDARD AUDIT PROCEDURE

Analytical analysis is an important tool auditors use to determine the reasonableness of sales. Comparing actual total sales to budget or historical amounts is useful in audit planning (see Project #1), but may not be a sufficient substantive test. Comparing sales to other data (e.g. sales per store or sales per square foot of retail space) or analyzing smaller subsets of total sales (e.g. sales by product line) can provide more useful insight regarding total sales. For companies having significant seasonal fluctuations, an analysis of seasonal sales is also an effective audit tool.

GATHERING EVIDENCE WITH DYNAMICS

Some of the items sold by SLI experience significant seasonal fluctuations. To facilitate analysis of these items, SLI classifies each inventory item into one of four item classes: Farm, Nursery, Pets, and Retail. Creating a chart (graph), such as Figure 13.1, that compares actual to projected seasonal sales for each item class can provide useful insight into sales patterns.

The chart shows that SLI expected to sell 10 percent of its total budgeted annual sales of standard items during the month of July. Actual reported sales in July exceeded 12 percent of actual annual sales.

Step 1: Obtain sales data for each inventory class.

Explorer can be used to prepare a list of all sales invoices. Because all sales-related transactions, including orders, quotes, and returns, are commingled with sales transactions, a search is required to select only invoice transactions for the fiscal year 2002.

The large number of transactions that will be selected in this search may exceed the ability of Explorer to export the list to Excel. Therefore, the search will be performed in two steps, selecting transactions from the first and last half of the fiscal year.

FIGURE 13.1
*Excel Chart of
Seasonal Sales*

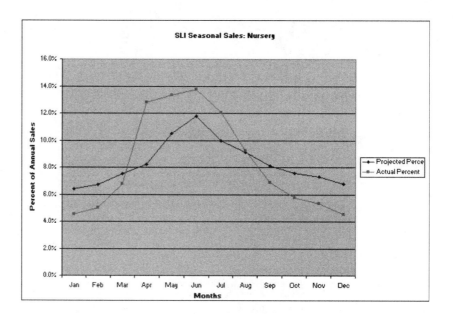

1 Select **Explorer >> Sales Line Items >> Default**.

2 Click **Columns** to remove the following columns: **SOP Number, Item Number, Item Description, QTY, Extended Cost, Unit Cost, Unit Price, Customer Number**.

3 Add the following columns: **Item Class Code, Document Date**.

4 Click **Search** to enter the following criteria:
a **SOP Type is equal to Invoice**
b **Document Date is between 1/1/2002 and 6/30/2002**

5 Enter **4000** in the Maximum Records box.
This process will take several minutes as the computer searches approximately 6,000 sales line items.

6 Click **Favorites** to save the view as **Audit Seasonal**.

7 Export the search results to **Excel**.
This process will also take several minutes. Do not perform other tasks on the computer during this process.

8 Save the spreadsheet as **SLI Monthly Sales**.

The sales line items for the first half of the year are now stored on a spreadsheet. Perform the following steps to obtain the sales line items for the second half of the year.

9 In Dynamics, click **Search**.

10 Modify the criteria dates to **between 7/01/2002 and 12/31/2002**.

11 Export the search results to **Excel**.

12 In Excel, copy the entire search results (excluding the column headings) below the search results on SLI Monthly Sales.

13 Save the revised spreadsheet.

To effectively copy a large area in Excel, first use the scroll bars to locate the cell in the lower right corner of the list. Click and drag from that cell up to A1.

The sales items for the entire year are now combined on SLI Monthly Sales and are ready for analysis.

Step 2: Prepare the data for charting.

Creating the chart in Figure 13.1 requires that sales be grouped by item class and month. These groupings can be calculated using Excel's PivotTable tool.

1 In Excel, click on any cell inside the list.

2 Select **Data >> PivotTable and PivotChart Report** to launch the PivotTable wizard.

3 Click Finish to view the structure of the PivotTable and the PivotTable toolbar shown in Figure 13.2.

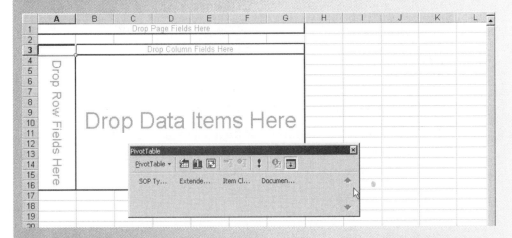

FIGURE 13.2
Excel PivotTable

4 Drag the **Document Date** button from the PivotTable toolbar and drop it in the Drop Row Fields Here area.
Pointing to a label on the PivotTable toolbar reveals its complete name.

5 Drop the **Item Class Code** button in the Drop Columns Fields Here area.

6 Drop the **Extended Price** button in Drop Data Items Here area.
You will not use the Drop Page Fields Here option in this application.

The PivotTable reports the total daily sales for each item class. To prepare the data for graphing, the sales should be grouped by month. The following steps show how to use Excel's grouping tool to modify the PivotTable.

7 Click on any date in the Document Date column.

8 Select **Data >> Group and Outline >> Group**.

9 Select **Months** and click **OK**.

10 Format the completed PivotTable in Currency,0 format.

11 Save the spreadsheet as **SLI Monthly Sales**.

A spreadsheet stored on the CD contains the structure for the table required to prepare the comparative chart. The spreadsheet also contains SLI's cyclical estimates for each item class. Monthly sales from the PivotTable will be copied to this spreadsheet. In the following instructions, you will create the chart for the Nursery item class.

12 Open the spreadsheet Chart.xls.

13 Switch to the SLI Monthly Sales spreadsheet.

14 Copy the monthly sales for Nursery as displayed in the PivotTable.

15 Switch to the Chart spreadsheet.

16 Paste the monthly sales in the Actual Sales column beginning at E6. *The formulas in column D divide each month's actual sales by the total annual sales calculated by the SUM function in E18.*

17 Copy the projected percentages for Nursery, found in the adjacent table, to column C of the analysis.

Step 3: Prepare a comparative chart.

The three data items required for the chart—month, projected percent, and actual percent—are now presented in adjacent cells, thus enabling Excel's chart wizard to create the chart.

1 Highlight the data in the Month, Projected Percent, and Actual Percent columns. Include the column headings, but not the totals.

2 Select **Insert >> Chart** to view the first window of the Chart Wizard in Figure 13.3.

3 Select **Line** in the Chart type box.

4 Select the **Line with markers** chart sub-type (second row, first column of the Chart sub-type box).

5 Click **Next** to view an example of the chart.

6 Click **Next** to view the window in Figure 13.4.

7 Enter **SLI Seasonal Sales: Nursery** in the Chart title box.

8 Enter **Months** in the Category (X) axis box.

9 Enter **Percent of Annual Sales** in the Category (Y) axis box.

10 Click **Next**.

11 Select the Radio button for **As new sheet**.

12 Click **Finish**.

13 Select **File >> Print** to print the chart.

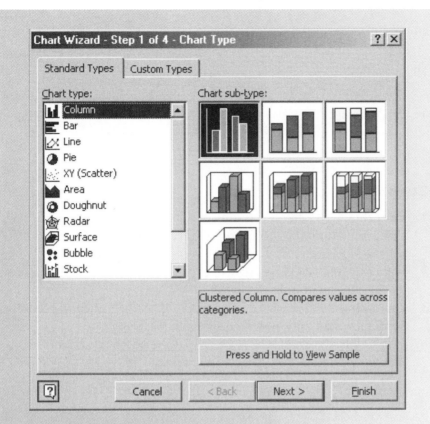

FIGURE 13.3

Excel Chart Wizard, Step 1 of 4

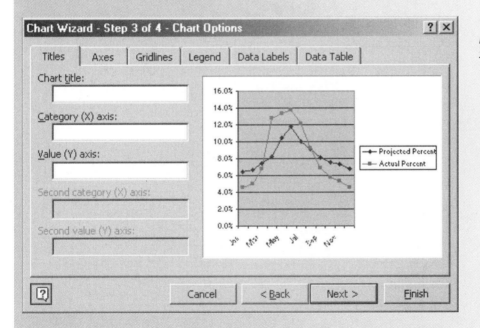

FIGURE 13.4

Excel Chart Wizard, Step 3 of 4

The chart shows the actual seasonal trend compared to management's expectations. Any significant deviations should be discussed with management and, if necessary, cause you to expand the audit scope of sales activity. Follow the steps to create a chart for the remaining three item classes.

14 Copy the monthly sales for the next item class from SLI Monthly Sales to Chart.

15 Copy the projected percent from the table. With new data inserted, the lines on the chart automatically change.

16 Click on the chart title to edit the title.

Questions

1 Print the PivotTable on the SLI Monthly Sales spreadsheet. Include a heading containing the client name, schedule description, and fiscal year end.

2 For each item class, print a line chart comparing actual and projected sales by month.

3 For each chart, prepare a summary of the significant differences between actual and budgeted sales.

Project #14
Sales Returns and Credits

AUDIT OBJECTIVE

Determine the existence, if any, of fraudulent activity related to sales return/credit transactions. Specifically, evaluate whether any excessive quantity or dollar value of credits have been issued by any employee or to any customer.

STANDARD AUDIT PROCEDURE

The auditor should quantify the number and amount of returns/credits issued by each employee to each customer. Any amounts that deviate from the normal activity should be investigated.

GATHERING EVIDENCE WITH DYNAMICS

Step 1: Evaluate the number of returns issued by each employee and to each customer.

Transactions for the return of merchandise are recorded using the sales transaction window. The customer is given a credit and the returned items are returned to inventory or discarded as damaged. Begin your search by using Explorer to create a list of return transactions containing the customer and employee names.

1 Select **Explorer >> Sales Transactions >> Default**.

2 Click **Columns** to remove the following columns: **SOP Number**, **Document Date**, **Customer PO Number**, **Primary Shipto Address Code**.

3 Add the **Posted User ID** column.
   The User ID entered when an employee logs into Dynamics is attached to every recorded sales transaction.

4 Click **Search** to enter the criteria **SOP Type is equal to Return**.

5 Click **Favorites** to save the view as **Audit Returns**.

6 Export the search results to **Excel**.

Excel's PivotTable feature can quickly analyze the data by customer and employee.

7 In Excel, position the cell pointer within the data.

8 Select **Data >> PivotTable and PivotChart Report** to launch the PivotTable wizard.

9 Click **Finish** to create the PivotTable. The structure of the PivotTable and the PivotTable toolbar appear, as shown in Figure 14.1.

FIGURE 14.1

Excel PivotTable

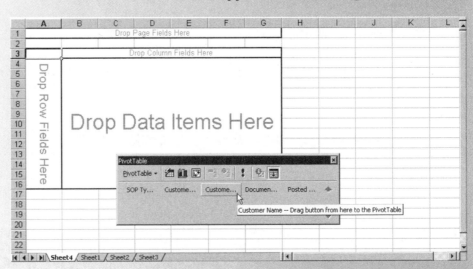

The PivotTable tool creates a table using the data in selected columns to identify the row and column headings of the table. The data within the table are calculated values, such as a sum or average, of the data in a third column. For this project, the PivotTable will calculate the sum of all sales returns issued to each customer by each employee. For example, management can quickly determine how much Mark Kelly had accepted in returns from Remington Contractors.

10 Drag the **Customer Name** button from the PivotTable toolbar and drop it in the Drop Row Fields Here area.
Point to each of the labels in the PivotTable toolbar to reveal its complete name.

11 Drag the **Posted User ID** button from the PivotTable toolbar and drop it in the Drop Columns Fields Here area.

12 Drag the **Document Amount** button from the PivotTable toolbar and drop it in the Drop Data Items Here area.
You will not use the Page options in this project.

13 Close the PivotTable window and format the completed PivotTable in Currency,2 format.

14 Save the spreadsheet as **Audit Returns**.

Examine the table to identify any unusual relationships. Under normal circumstances, you would expect the amount of returns processed by each employee to be relatively consistent with other employees. Refunds issued by an employee to a single customer that that appear unusually high also should be investigated.

Step 2: Evaluate the number of returns issued to a customer.

The PivotTable reports the dollar amount of returns for each customer. Before examining individual transactions for any customer, you should determine that customer's level of returns relative to sales by calculating a return rate. In the following steps, you will calculate a return ratio for PWC Farming, Inc.

1 In Dynamics, select **Inquiry >> Sales >> Receivables Summ**.

2 Enter **1111** in the From box.

3 Click **Calculate**. A screen similar to Figure 14.2 will appear.

FIGURE 14.2 *Receivables Summary Inquiry*

Number	Type	Original Amount	Unapplied Amount
16	Sales	$11,093.35	$1,419.71
0	Installments	$0.00	$0.00
8	Finance Charges	$217.22	$0.00
0	Debit Memos	$0.00	$0.00
0	Service / Repairs	$0.00	$0.00
0	Warranties	$0.00	$0.00
0	Credit Memos	$0.00	$0.00
4	Returns / Credits	$1,706.84	$1,127.10
5	Cash Receipts	$9,890.86	$0.00
	Totals	-$287.13	$292.61

Open Item as last aged:

Period	Amount
0-30 Days	-$569.61
31 - 60 Days	$359.97
61 - 90 Days	$0.00
91 and Over	$502.25

Balance forward as last consolidated:

Period	Amount
Current	$0.00
Non-Current	$0.00

The return rate for PWC Farming, Inc. is calculated by dividing the returns/credits of $1,706.84 by total sales of $11,093.35. A rate that is above a normal return rate would cause you to investigate further.

Step 3: Examine individual return transactions.

Having determined that the return activity of a particular customer needs further investigation, you should examine some of the individual transactions. Follow these steps to examine a return transaction for PWC Farming, Inc.

1 Select **Inquiry >> Sales >> Trx by Customer**.

2 Enter **1111** as the Customer ID.

3 Scroll down the list to locate the **RTN** transactions in the Type column.

4 Highlight the **INV0078** transaction.

5 Click **Document Number** to examine the transaction details.

6 Click **Show** to examine the items returned.

7 Click **Distributions** to determine if the inventory items were returned to inventory.

A returned item that is salable is returned to the inventory, resulting in a debit entry to account 000-1300-00, Inventory. Damaged inventory is thrown away, resulting in a debit entry to account 000-4520-00, Cost of Goods Sold—Shrinkage. You should evaluate the inventory items returned and damaged, as well as the frequency of these transactions, in concluding whether any fraudulent activity may exist.

Questions

1 Print the PivotTable report of returns by customer and employee. The report should include the client name, report description, and audit fiscal year.

2 Which employee issued the greatest amount of refunds? What was the total amount?

3 Which customer received the greatest amount of refunds? What was the total amount?

4 Identify the most unusual employee/customer combination. What portion of the total refunds to all customers were issued to by this employee to this customer?

5 Identify the number of sales and returns/credit transactions of customers 1111, PWC Farming, Inc, and 6620, Remington Contractors. Calculate a return rate for each customer.

6 Evaluate the individual return transactions for Remington Contractors. Were these items returned to the inventory or written off as damaged? Can you detect any evidence that might lead you to believe a fraud has been committed?

Project #15

Authorized Sales Prices

Determine that authorized sales prices were used to price sales transactions.

STANDARD AUDIT PROCEDURE

The unit sales prices on a sales invoice are compared to the authorized price list. Auditors performing this task in a traditional accounting system would be required to audit only a sample of these transactions. Performing this audit procedure using Dynamics, however, enables the auditor to expand the test beyond a sample to the entire population of sales invoices.

SLI did not activate an optional Dynamics security feature that prevents employees authorized to make sales from altering the unit sales prices on individual sales invoices. The Board of Directors has requested that the audit include an examination of the unit sales prices used to price items sold to credit customers.

GATHERING EVIDENCE WITH DYNAMICS

Step 1: Export the relevant data from Dynamics to Excel.

Explorer contains three searches that will be useful in gathering the data necessary to perform this audit procedure. The data will first be exported to Excel and then transferred to Access to complete the analysis.

The first task is to obtain a list of sales invoices (excluding those for the point-of-sales system, account 9999) that includes the name of the employee who entered the transaction. Dynamics automatically stores the user ID for each sales transaction. Because all sales related transactions, including orders, quotes, and returns, are commingled with sales transactions, the search must include a criteria to select only sales invoices.

1 Select **Explorer >> Sales Transactions >> Default**.

2 Click **Columns** to remove the following columns: **Document Date**, **Customer PO Number**, **Primary Shipto Address Code**.

3 Add the **Posted User ID** column.

4 Click **Search** to enter the following criteria:
  a **SOP Type is equal to Invoice**
  b **Customer Number is not equal to 9999**

5 Click **Favorites** to save the view as **Audit Sales Trans**.

6 Export the search results to **Excel**.

7 Save the Excel spreadsheet as **SLI Sales**.

The second task is to obtain a list of all items sold on these sales invoices.

8 Select **Explorer >> Sales Line Items >> Default**.

9 Click **Columns** to remove the following columns: **QTY**, **Extended Cost**, **Extended Price**, **Unit Cost**.

10 Click **Search** to enter the following criteria:
  a **SOP Type is equal to Invoice**
  b **Customer Number is not equal to 9999**

11 Enter **6000** in the Maximum Records box.
  This process will take several minutes as the computer searches approximately 6,000 sales line items.

12 Click **Favorites** to save the view **Audit Items**.

13 Export the search results to **Excel**.

14 Save the Excel spreadsheet as **SLI Items**.
  This process will take several minutes. Do not perform other tasks on the computer during this process.

The final task is to obtain a list of the employees.

15 Select **Explorer >> Employees >> Default**.

16 Click **Columns** to remove the following columns: **Address 1**, **Address 2**, **City**, **State**, **Zip**, **Phone 1**.

17 Add the **User ID** column.

18 Click **Favorites** to save the view as **Audit Employees**.

19 Export the search results to **Excel**.

20 Save the Excel spreadsheet as **SLI Employees**.

Step 2: Export the data from Excel to Access.

The structure of the data required for this audit procedure makes the use of an Access database a better analysis tool than Excel. The search results currently contained on the three Excel spreadsheets can easily be copied into Access. Begin your analysis by creating a blank Access database.

1 Launch Access from your desktop.
Or select Start >> Programs >> Microsoft Access.

2 Select **Blank Access database**.

3 Click **OK**.

4 Enter the file name **Audit SLI**.

5 Click **Create** to view the Access Database window in Figure 15.1.

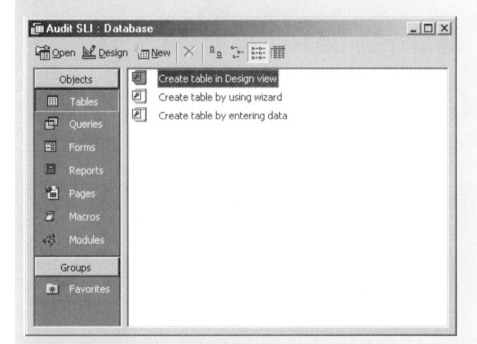

Access is a better analysis tool than Excel when (1) the data are stored in multiple locations or (2) the number of records may exceed the RAM capacity of your computer.

FIGURE 15.1
Access Database Window

The data on each Excel spreadsheet will be copied into an Access table.

6 Switch to the Excel spreadsheet **Audit Sales**.

7 Highlight the search results.

8 Select **Edit >> Copy**.

9 Switch to Access.

10 In Access, select **Edit >> Paste**.

11 Select **Yes** at the prompt "Does the first row of your data contain column headings?"

12 Click **OK** to confirm that Access "Successfully imported Sheet1."

13 With Sheet1 highlighted, select **Edit >> Rename**.

14 Change the table name to **Sales** and press **Enter**.

15 Repeat steps 6-14 for the remaining two spreadsheets, naming the tables **Items** and **Employees**.

Access is a relational database. Access stores data in tables that resemble an Excel spreadsheet. Each column of a table is a field, such as item number, quantity, etc. Each row is a record, such as all the data for inventory item 832-1123.

An Access select query is used to bring the data together in a single dynaset.

16 Click **Queries** in the Objects area.

17 Double-click on **Create query in Design view** to display the Show Table window in Figure 15.2.

FIGURE 15.2

Access Show Table WIndow

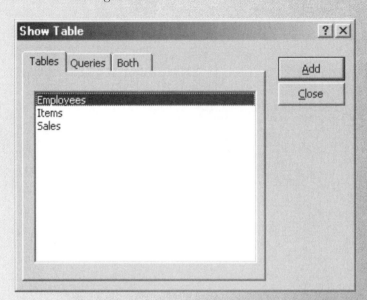

A dynaset is a subgroup of data from one or more tables. The Access select query lets you select data from more than one data source, including tables and other queries. Queries also enable you to sort and filter data.

18 Select **Items** and click **Add**.

19 Select **Sales** and click **Add**.

20 Select **Employees** and click **Add**.

21 Click **Close** to display the query design shown in Figure 15.3.

FIGURE 15.3

Access Query Design Window

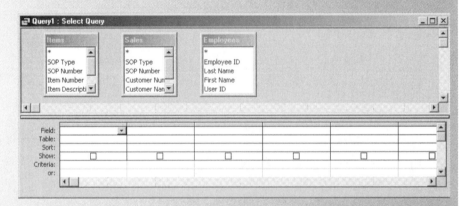

The three boxes in the top portion of the window show the fields located in each table. The bottom portion of the window is used to select the fields to be included in the query results. To operate properly, selected fields in the three tables must be linked with relationships.

22 Click on **SOP Number** in the Items table.

23 Click and drag SOP Number and drop it on SOP Number in the Sales table. A line will be drawn between the two SOP Number fields.

24 Click on **Posted User ID** in the Sales table.
You may have to use the scroll bar to find the field.

25 Click and drag Posted User ID and drop it on the User ID field in the Employees table. A line will be drawn between the two fields. Your query will now appear as shown in the top section of Figure 15.4

The fields to be included in the dynaset are selected next.

26 Double-click on the fields from the following table. As you double-click each field, the field name will appear in the lower portion of the select query, as shown in Figure 15.4.

Field	Table
SOP Number	Sales
Customer Number	Sales
Customer Name	Sales
Item Number	Items
Item Description	Items
Unit Price	Items
Last Name	Employees

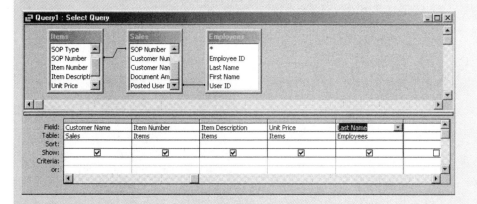

FIGURE 15.4
Access Select Query Design

27 Click the **View** button, , on the toolbar to view query results.

The select query has brought related data from three tables together in a single dynaset. The dynaset resembles a table of data in that it can be used as a data source for any analysis.

28 Close the window.

29 Click **Yes** to save the query changes.

30 Save the query as **Sales Items**.

Step 3: Create an Access crosstab query to analyze unit sales prices.

All the data required to analyze unit sales prices is now in one dynaset named Sales Items. The data is now ready to be analyzed using an Access crosstab query. The crosstab query is a useful tool for analyzing relationships between several items of data.

1 In Access, select **Queries >> New**.

2 Select **Crosstab Query Wizard** and click **OK**. The first screen of the wizard appears, as shown in Figure 15.5.

FIGURE 15.5

Access Crosstab Query Wizard (Window 1)

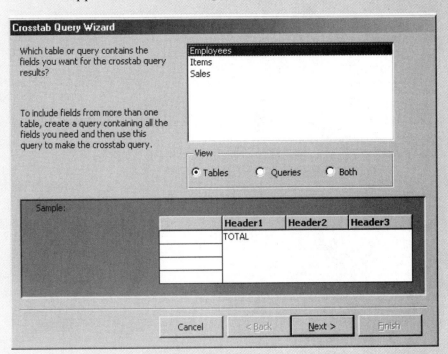

3 Click the **Queries** radio button in the View area. The Sales Items query should appear in the upper window. Because there is only one query in the list, it is automatically selected.

4 Click **Next** to display the second wizard window in Figure 15.6.

5 Select **Item Number** in the Available Fields box and click **Insert** to select the field.

6 Select **Item Description** in the Available Fields box and click **Insert** to select the field.
The query will use the data in the Item Number and Item Description fields to create the row headings.

7 Click **Next**.

8 Select **Last Name** for the column headings.
The query will use the data in the Last Name field to create the column headings.

The Access crosstab query is similar to the Excel PivotTable used in two other projects in this book. The crosstab query creates a table using the data in selected columns to identify the rows and columns headings of a table.

FYI

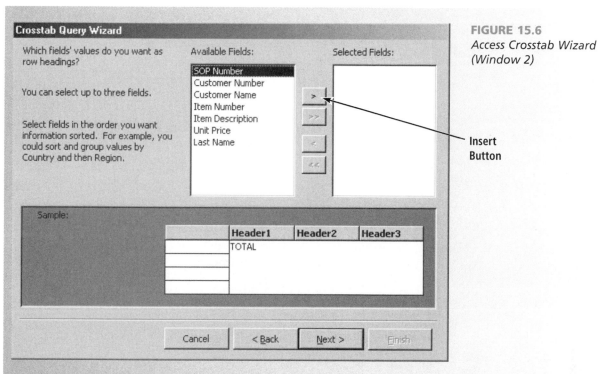

FIGURE 15.6
Access Crosstab Wizard (Window 2)

9 Click **Next**.

10 Select **Unit Price** in the Fields box.

11 Click **Min** in the Functions box to calculate the minimum unit price of each item. Your window should now appear as shown in Figure 15.7.

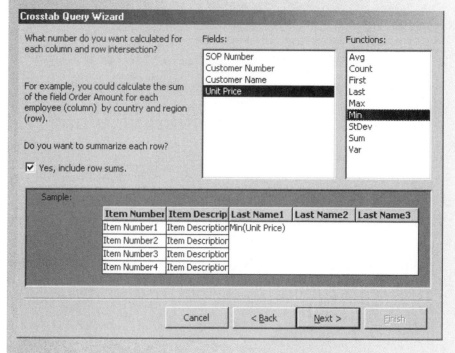

FIGURE 15.7
Access Crosstab Wizard (Window 3)

FYI

Employees may commit a sales fraud for a variety of reasons. An employee may give a friend a discount as a personal favor. An unethical customer may pay a kickback to an employee for selling items at a discount. The minimum unit sales price is examined here in an attempt to identify items sold at a discount. However, if an item's unit sales price is reduced, any unauthorized discounts off the original price may not be detected. Thus, this test can quickly detect improper discounts by an employee, but does not provide absolute assurance that no fraudulent activity has occurred.

12 Select **Next >> Finish** to display the crosstab query shown in Figure 15.8.

FIGURE 15.8

Access Crosstab Results

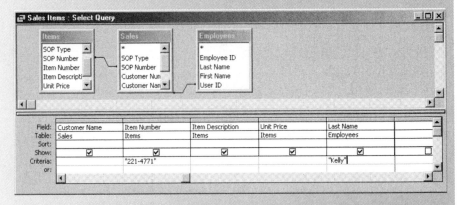

Item Number	Item Descriptio	Total Of Unit P	Clark	Jensen	Kelly	Matthews
104-6300	Wheelbarrow	$89.99	$89.99		$89.99	
104-6309	Sprayer	$159.99	$159.99	$159.99	$159.99	
113-2749	Peat Moss -- 6	$9.95	$9.95	$9.95	$9.95	
113-2755	Potting Soil -- 4l	$4.95	$4.95	$4.95	$4.95	
113-2763	Top Soil -- 40 lb	$1.49	$1.49	$1.49	$1.49	
113-7632	Dog Treats	$0.15			$0.15	
113-7654	Dog Food -- 50	$7.95	$7.95	$7.95	$7.95	
113-7694	Cat Food -- 25 l	$12.95	$12.95	$12.95	$12.95	
221-4762	Pea Seed	$0.18			$0.18	
221-4769	Corn	$0.79	$0.79	$0.79	$0.79	$0.79
221-4771	Bean	$0.17	$0.19	$0.19	$0.17	$0.19
256-2004	Enviro-Shade La	$0.19		$0.19	$0.19	
256-2005	Centipede Seed	$3.25	$3.25	$3.25	$3.25	

Notice that Kelly sold a sprayer for item 221-4771, bean seed, for $0.17 while the other employees sold the item for $0.19. The auditor should investigate the reason for this difference.

13 Click the **Print** button, 🖨, to print the query results.

14 Close the crosstab query window.

The following steps will show you how to modify the Sales Items select query to enter the criteria to select 221-4771 sales by Kelly.

15 Select **Queries >> Sales Items >> Design**.

16 Enter **221-4771** in the Criteria line in the Item Number column.

17 Enter **Kelly** in the Criteria line of the Last Name column. Your query layout should appear as shown in Figure 15.9.

FIGURE 15.9

Query Layout Using Criteria

18 Click the **View** button, ▦, on the toolbar to view query results.

19 Click the **Print** button, 🖨, to print the query results.

The query results show all the sales of that inventory item sold by Kelly. Any differences in prices charged to any customer should be noted and investigated. By changing the data in the criteria line, the query can be used repeatedly to search for any combination of inventory item and employee name.

20 Close the window without saving the changes.

21 When you finish using Access, click the **Close** button.

Questions

1 Print the first page of the SLI Sales, SLI Items, and SLI Employees spreadsheets. Because these spreadsheets are used to create Access data tables, do not enter a heading.

2 Create the crosstab query that shows the minimum unit sales price by customer and employee. Print the query.

3 Use the crosstab query to identify three inventory items that one employee sold at a price below the price sold by other employees. For each instance,

   a Create and print a query that shows the unit prices by customer. (You can modify the column widths of an Access query in the same manner as you do Excel columns, enabling the query to print on a single page.)

   b Identify if the lower sales price is focused on any particular customer.

Index